THE (TRUE!) HISTORY OF ART

Thank you to Laurent P. for his mind-blowing idea, Alexis for his talent, and the whole team at Palette.
Sylvain C.

SYLVAIN COISSARD • ALEXIS LEMOINE

THE (TRUE!) HISTORY OF ART

SELF MADE HERO

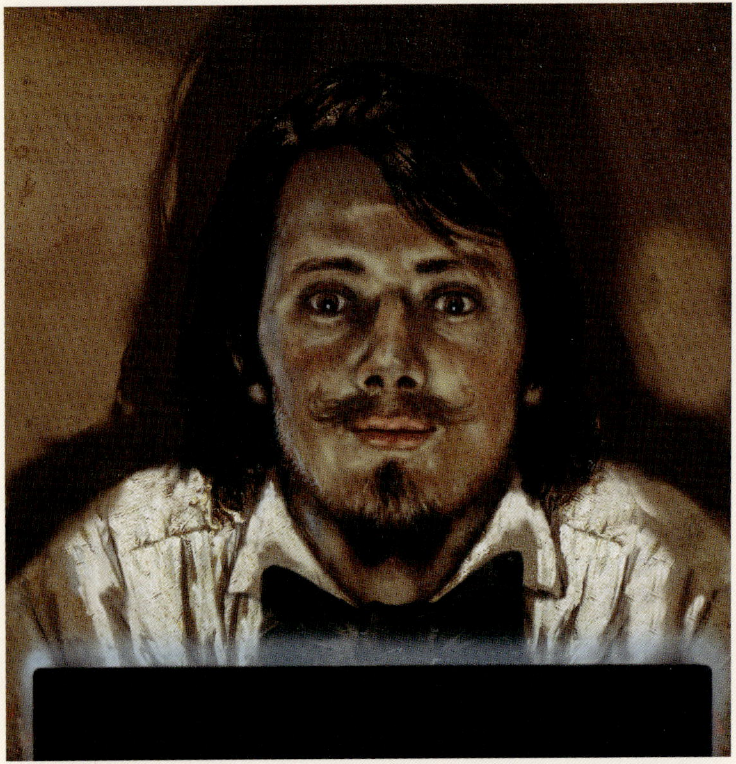

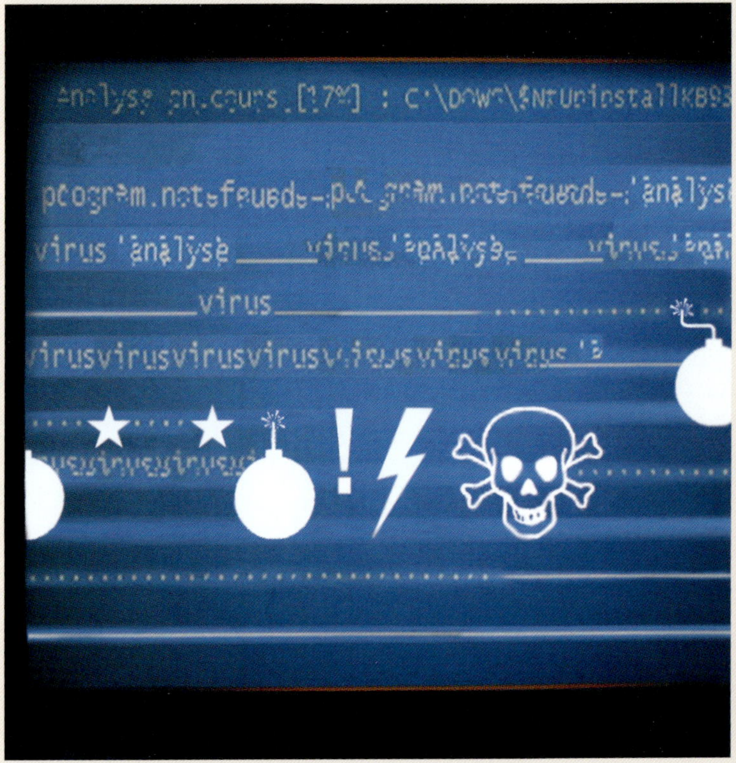
virus
virusvirusvirusvirus

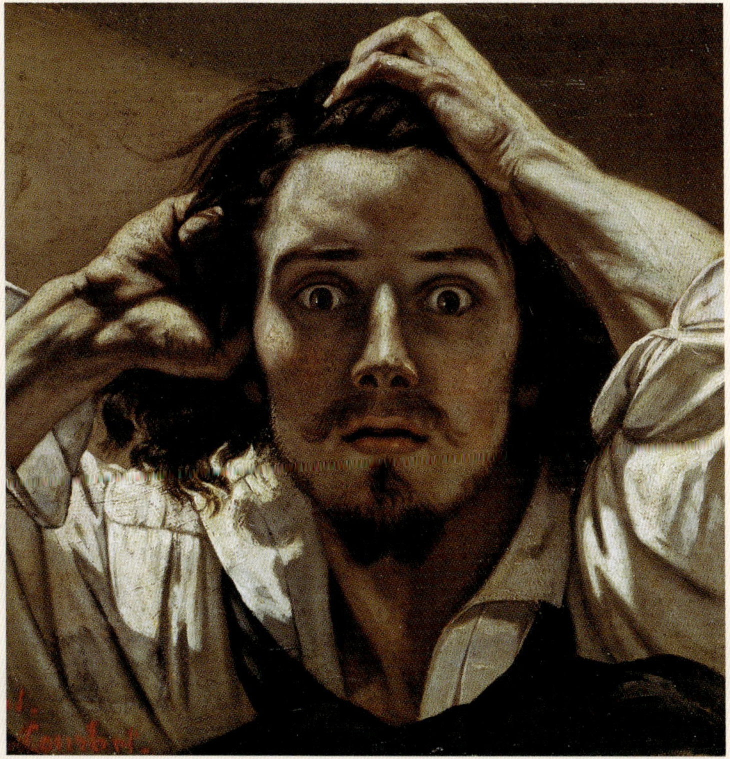

Gustave Courbet, *The Desperate Man*, 1841.

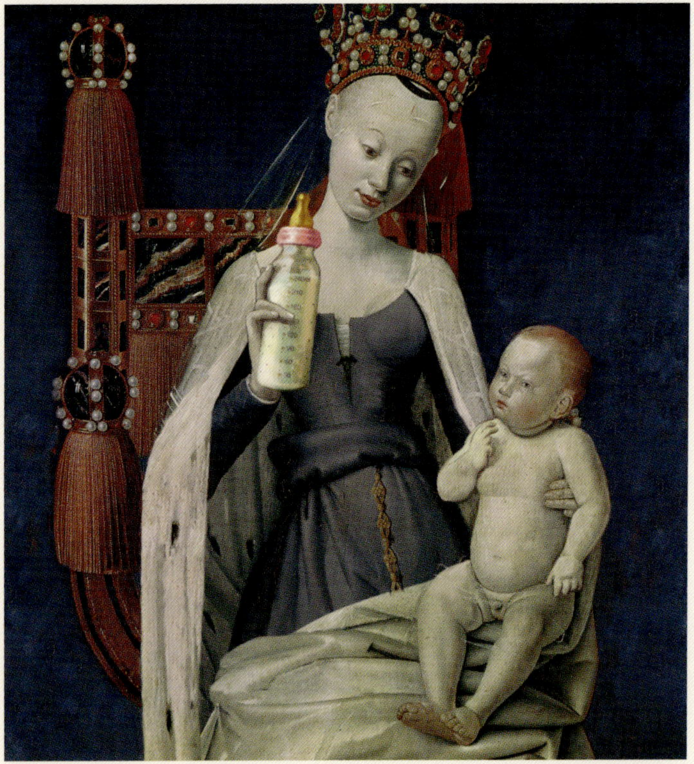

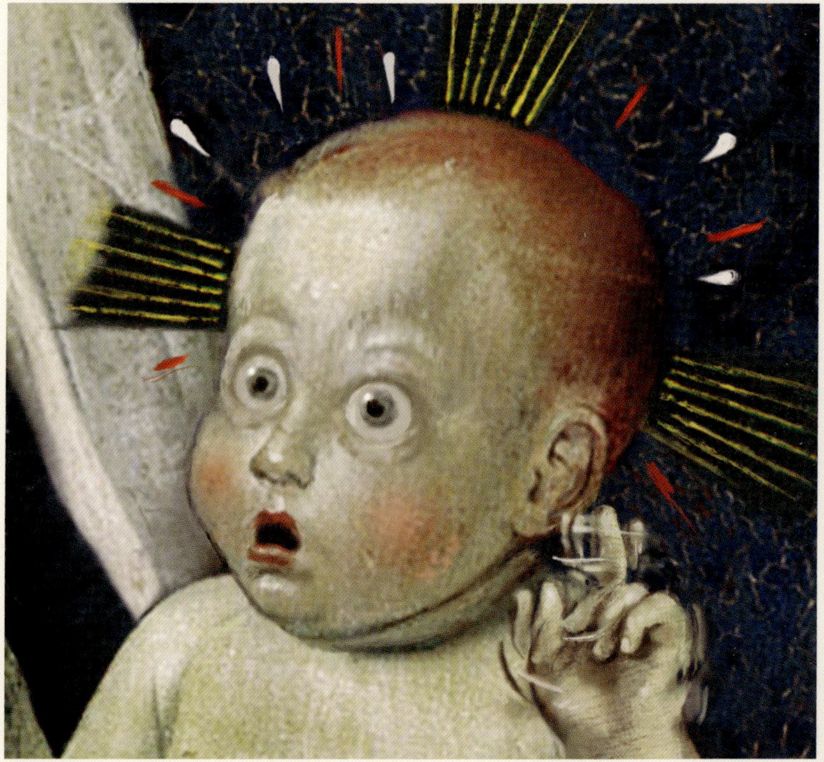

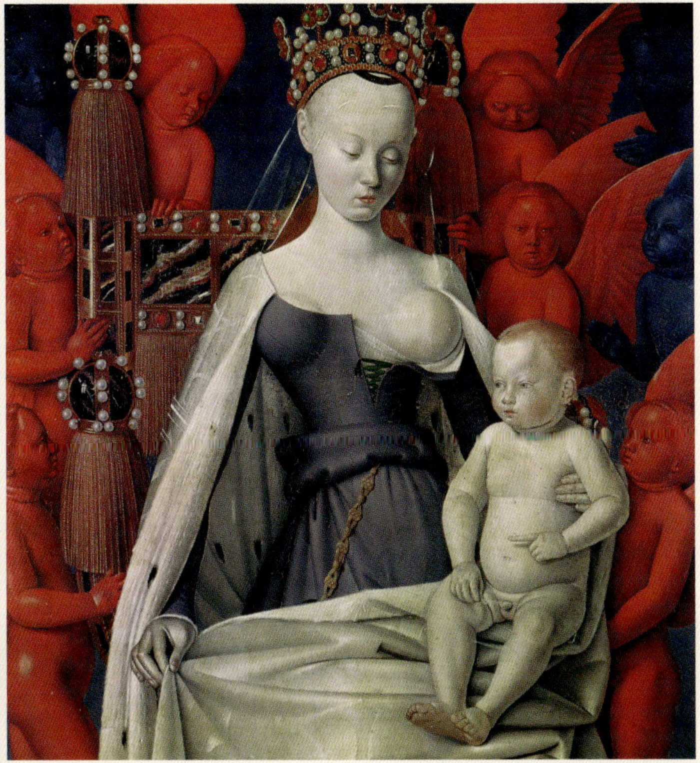

Jean Fouquet, *Virgin and Child Surrounded by Angels*, 1452.

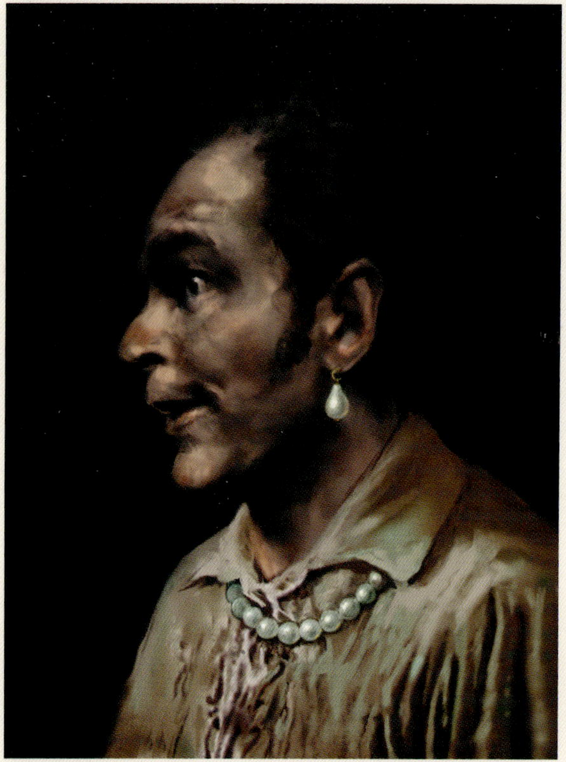

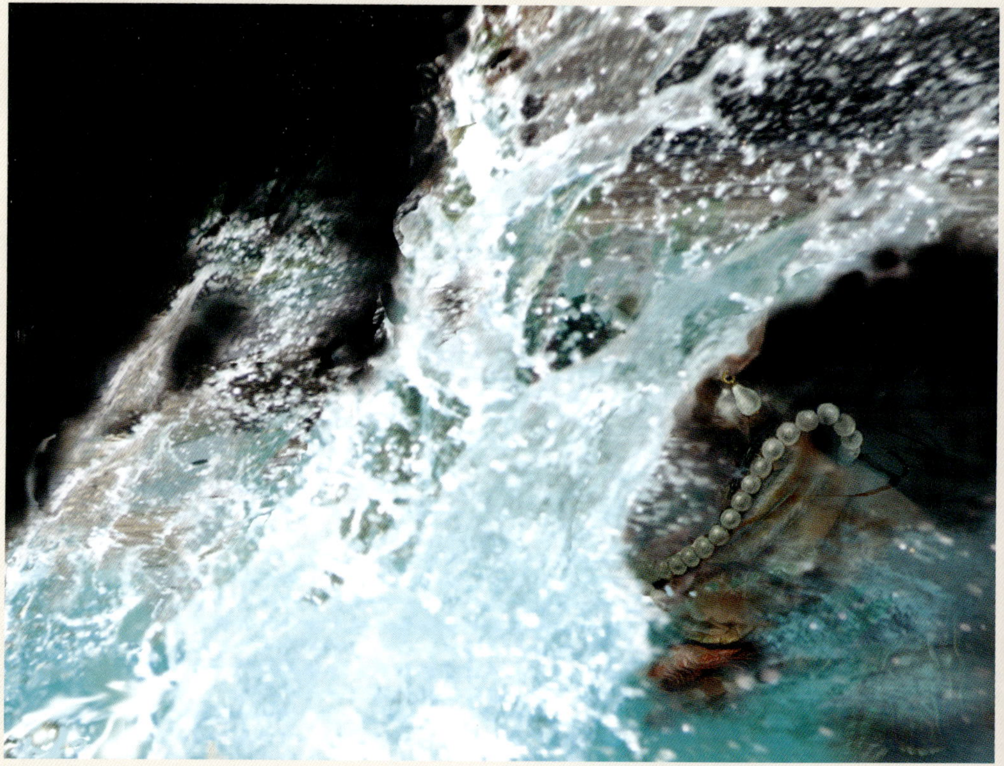

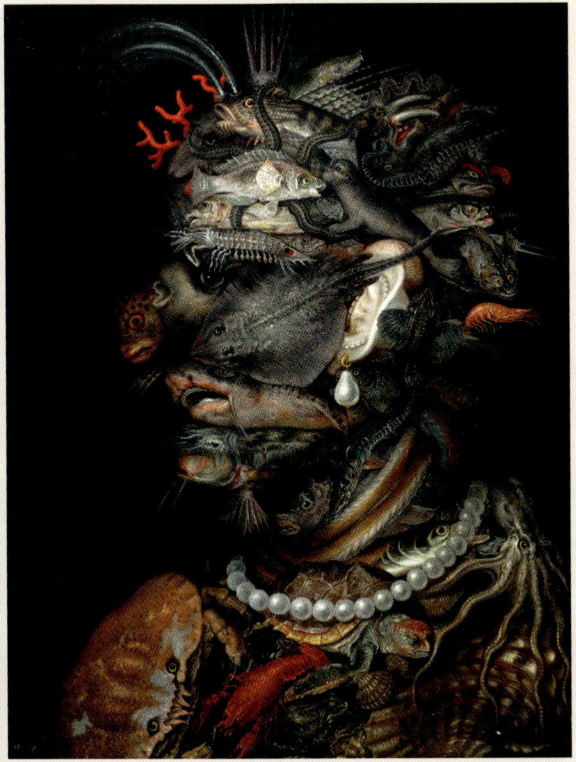

Giuseppe Arcimboldo, *Water*, 1566.

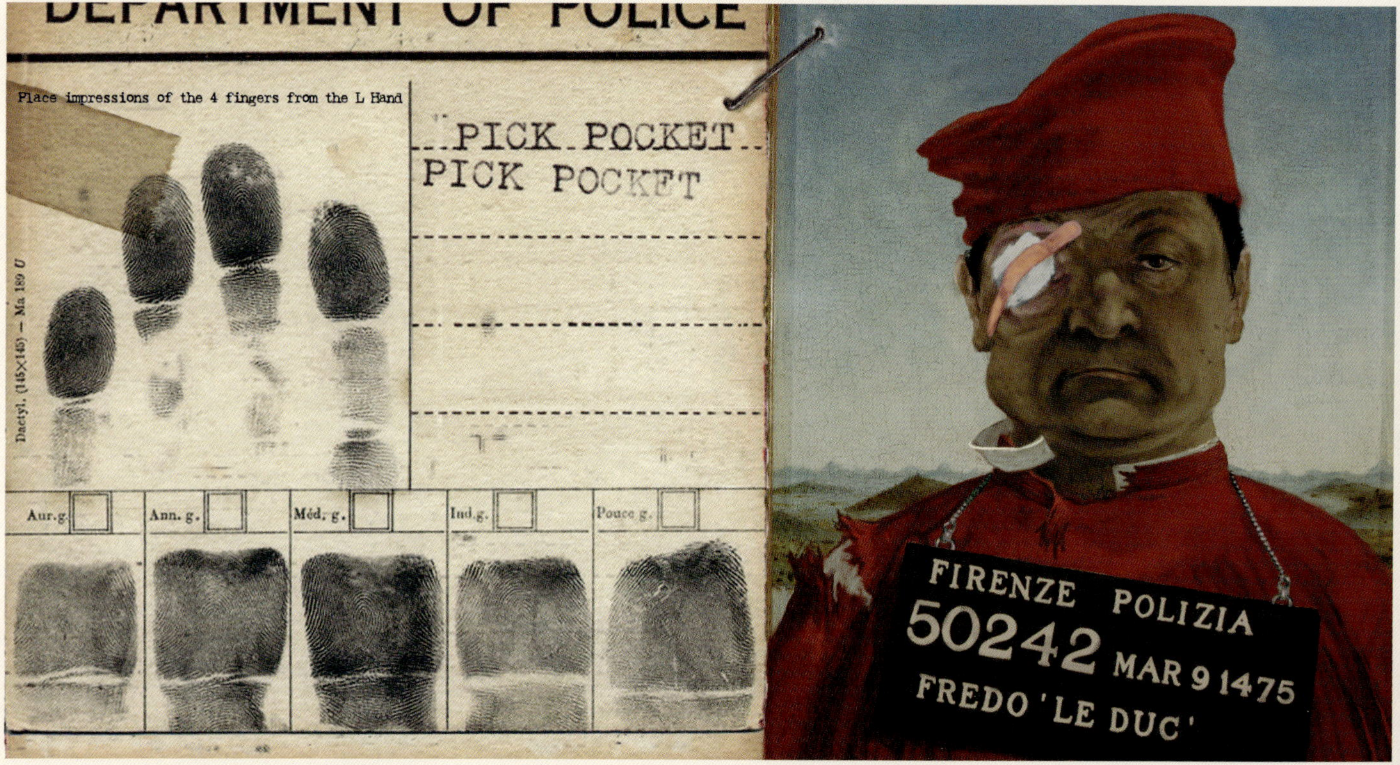
DEPARTMENT OF POLICE
Place impressions of the 4 fingers from the L Hand
PICK POCKET
PICK POCKET
Aur.g.
Ann. g.
Méd. g.
Ind.g.
Pouce g.
FIRENZE POLIZIA
50242 MAR 9 1475
FREDO 'LE DUC'

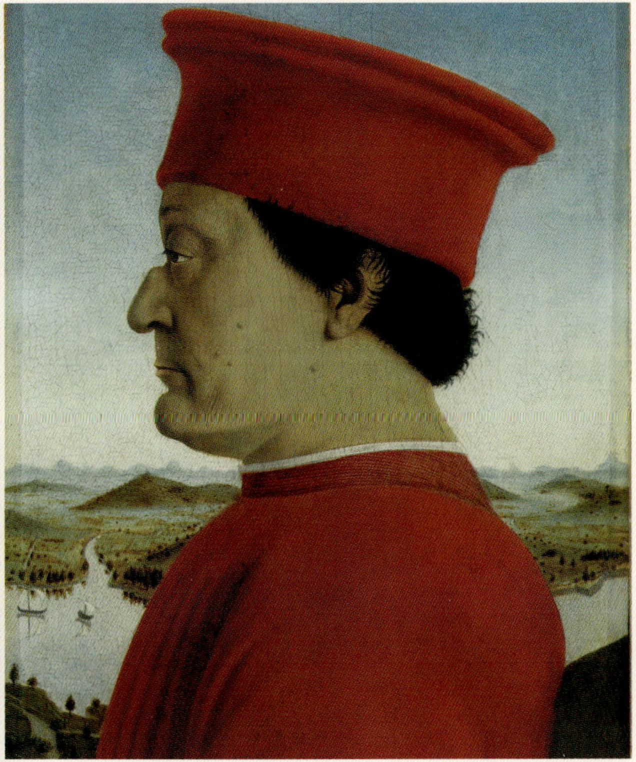

Piero della Francesca, *Federico III da Montefeltro*, 1464–1466.

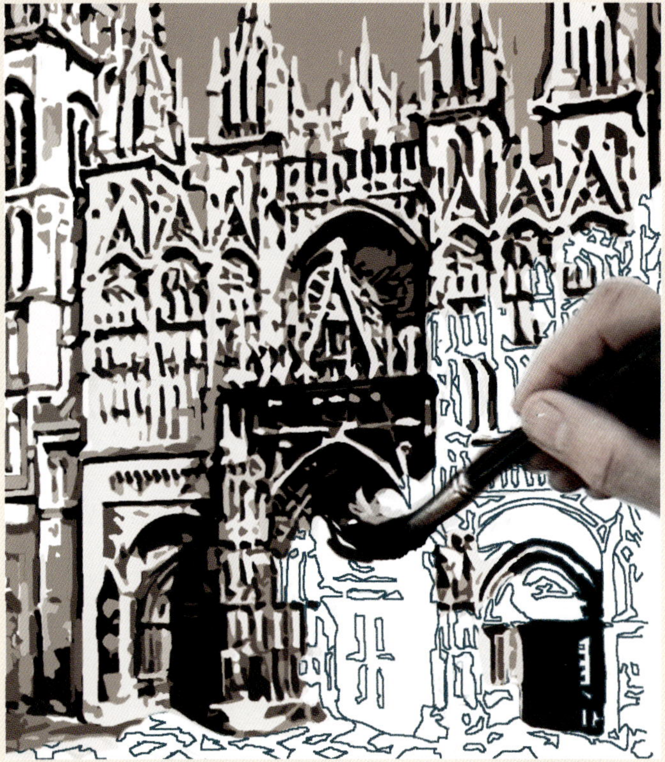

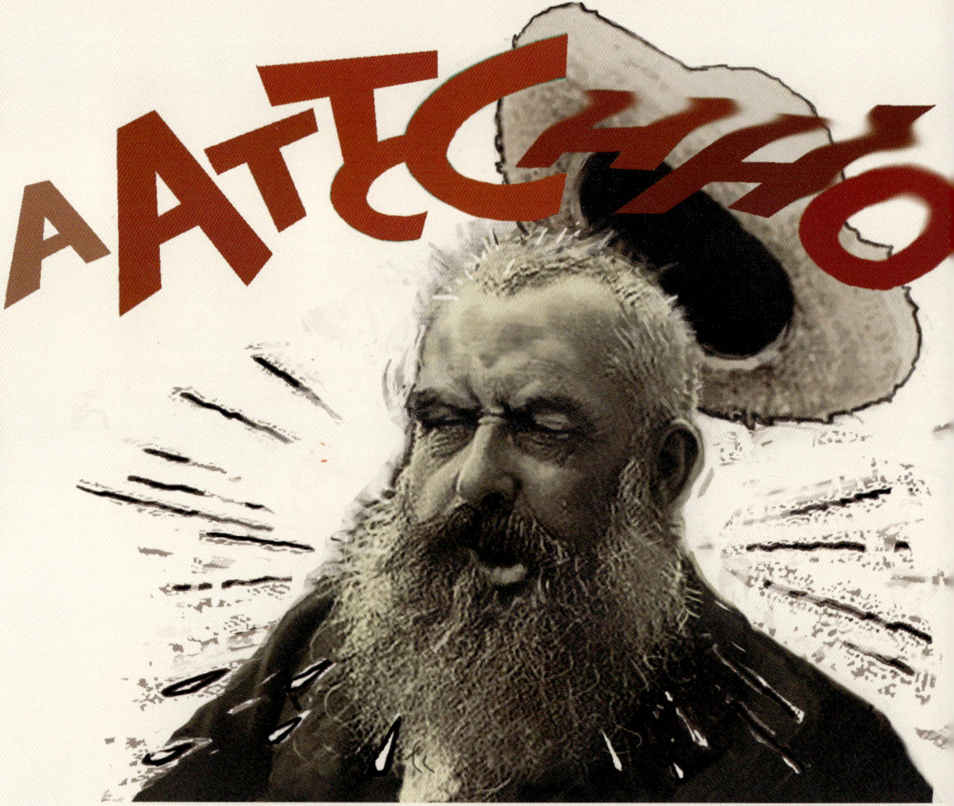
AATTCCHO

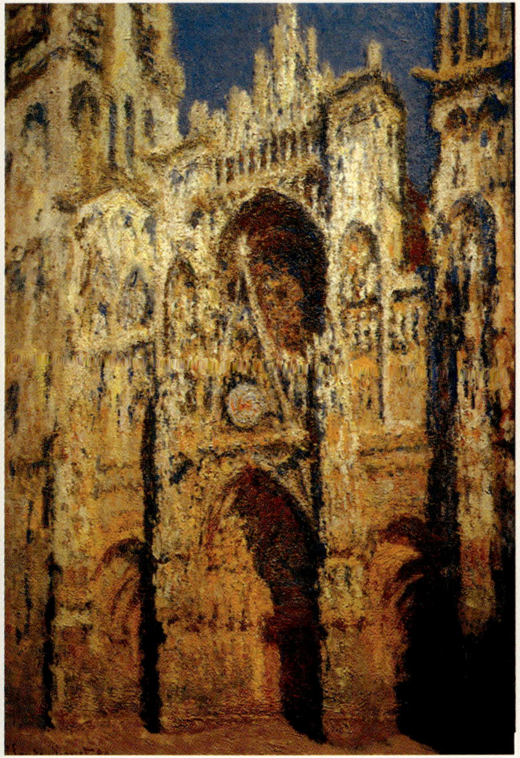

Claude Monet, *Rouen Cathedral: The Portal in the Sunlight*, 1893.

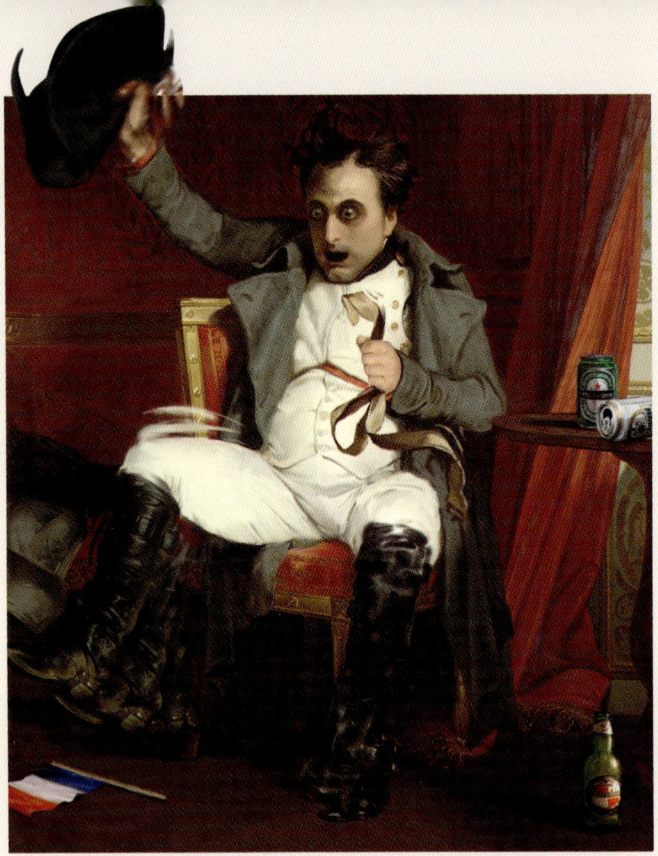

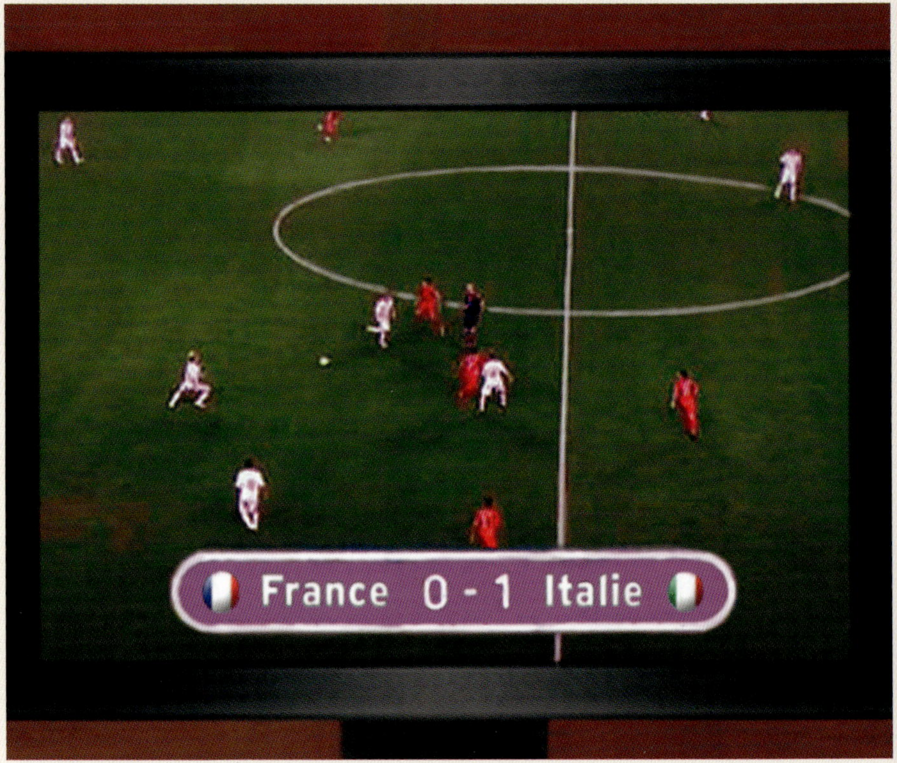
France 0 - 1 Italie

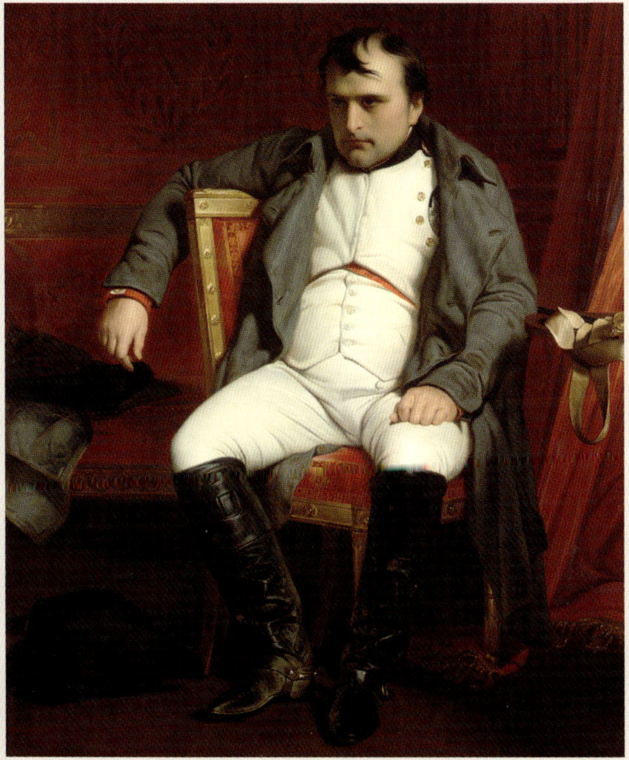

Paul Delaroche, ***Napoleon I at Fontainebleau on 31st March 1814*****, 1840.**

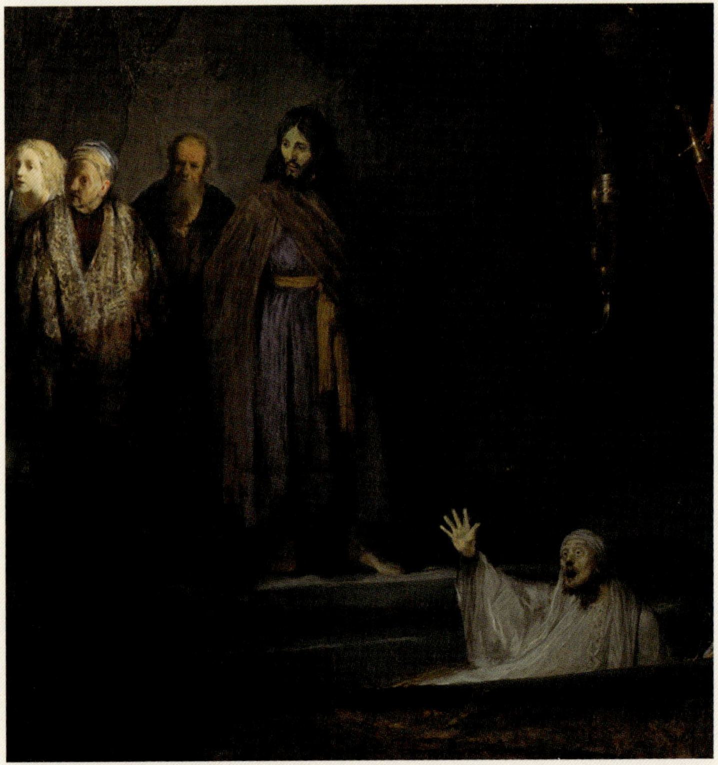

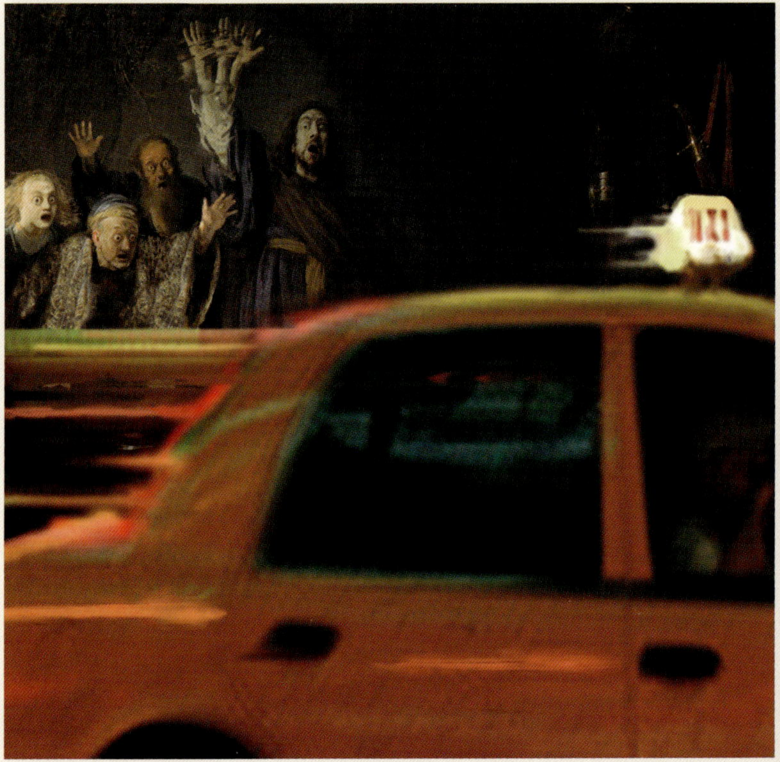

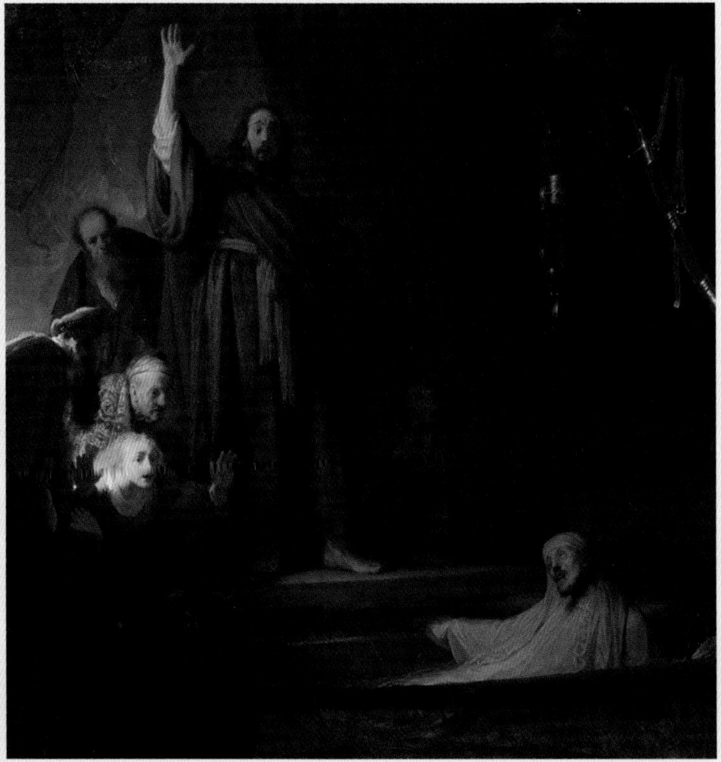

Rembrandt, *The Raising of Lazarus*, c. 1630.

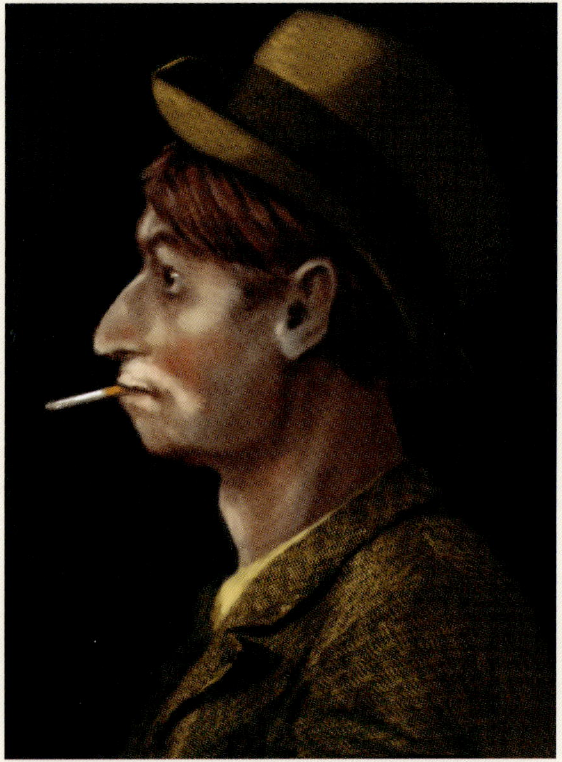

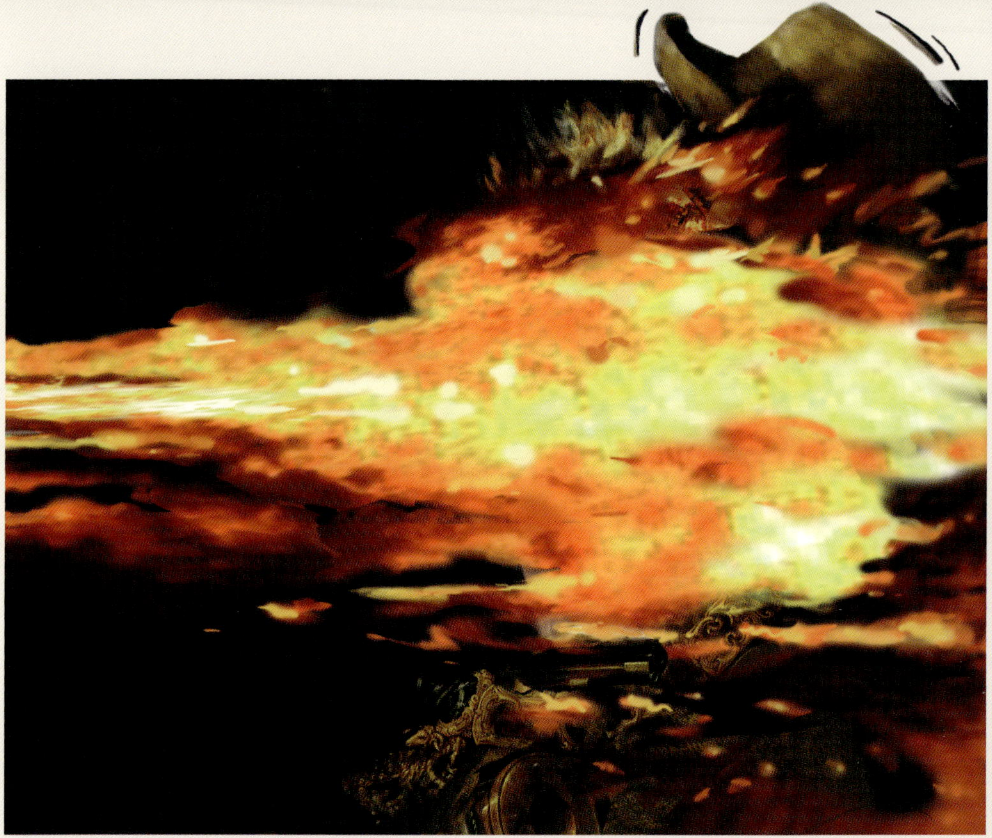

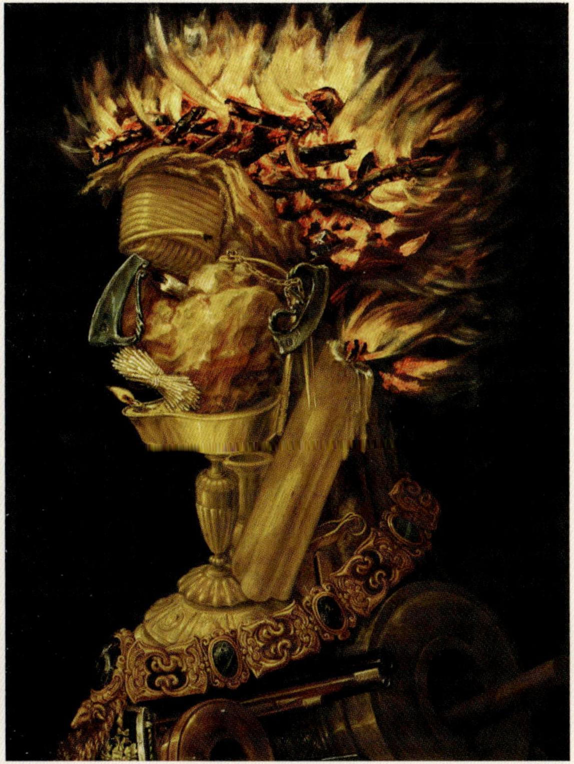

Giuseppe Arcimboldo, *Fire*, 1566.

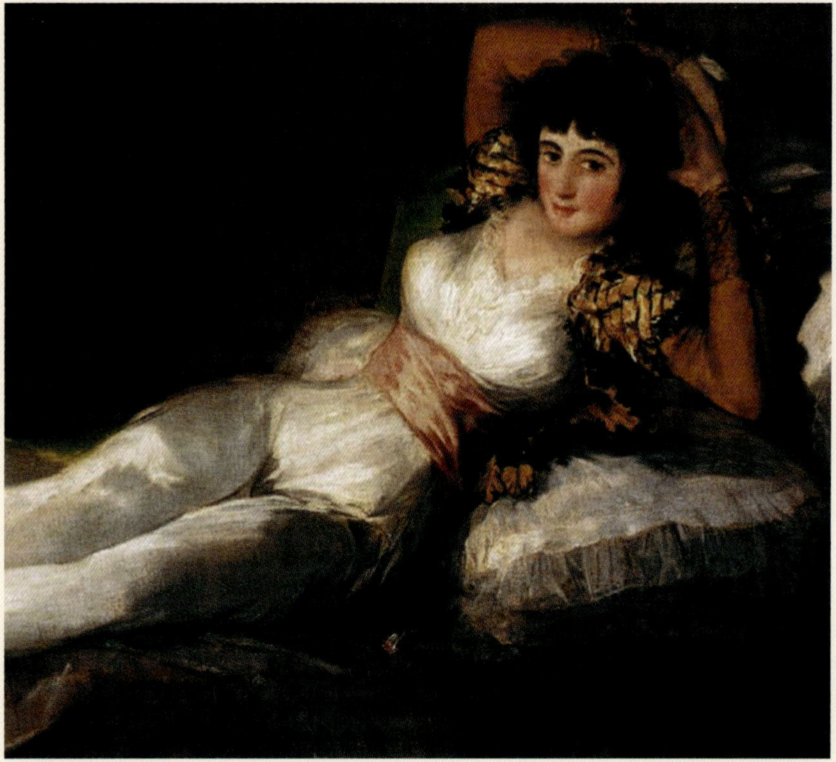

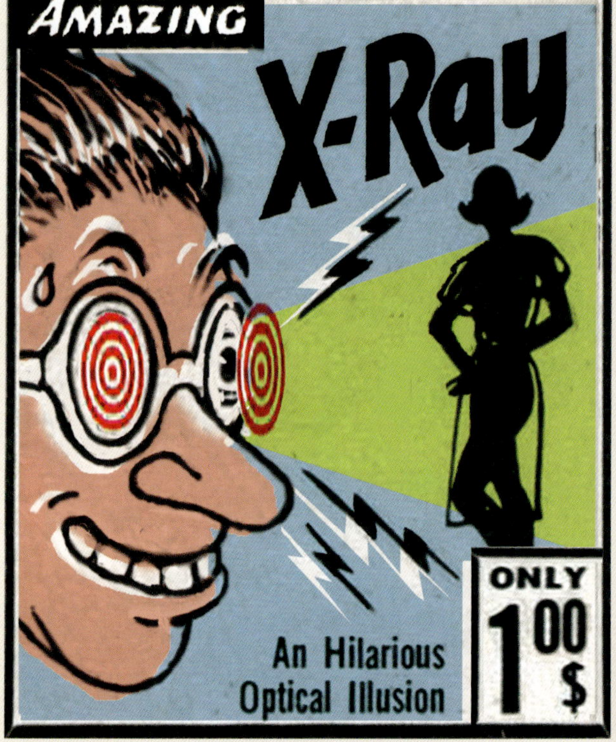
AMAZING
X-Ray
ONLY
1.00 $
An Hilarious
Optical Illusion

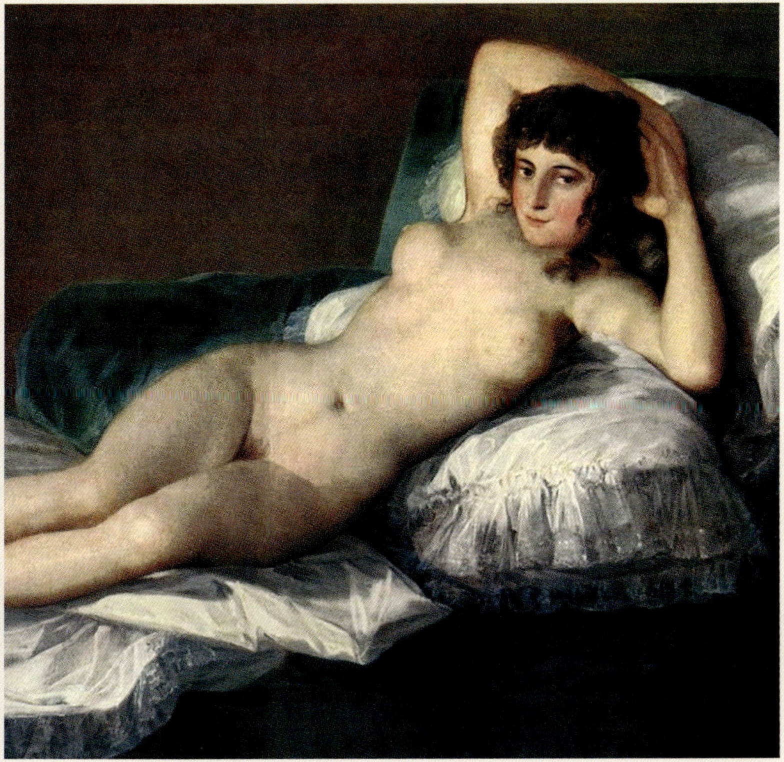

Francisco de Goya, *The Clothed Maja*, *The Nude Maja*, 1800-1803.

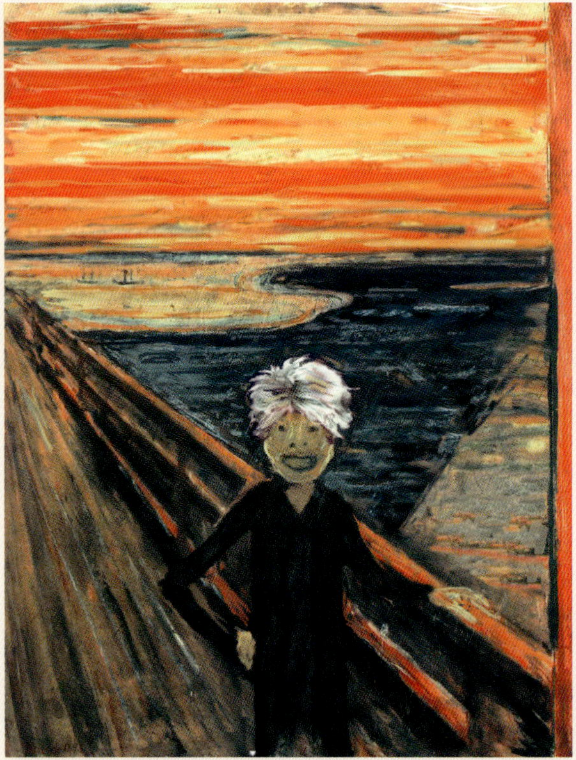

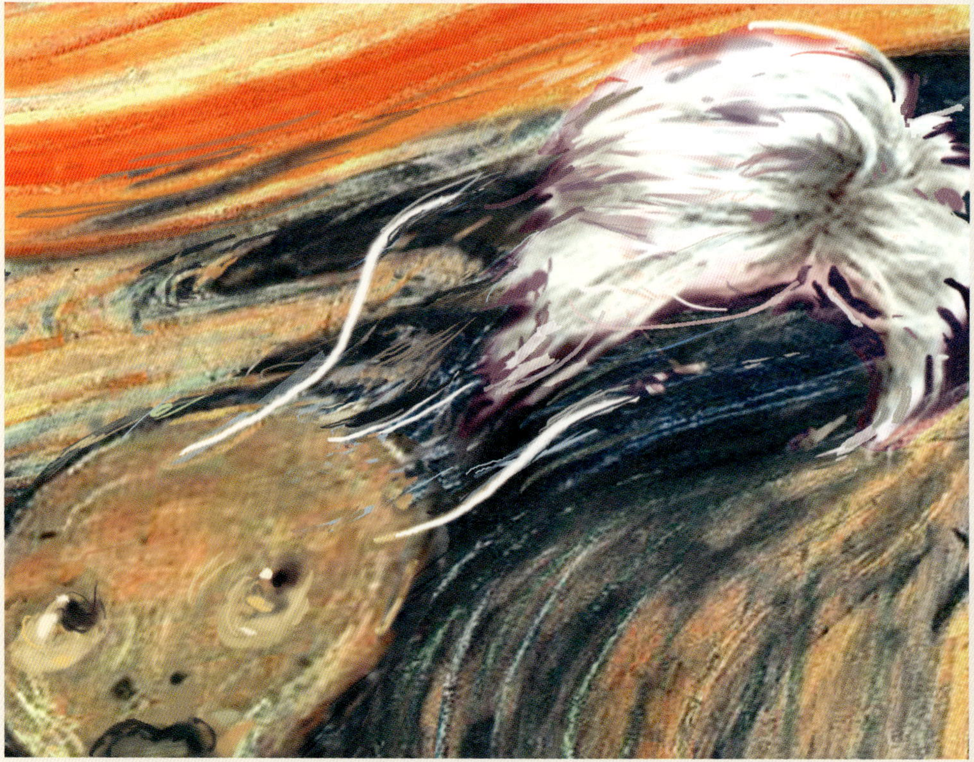

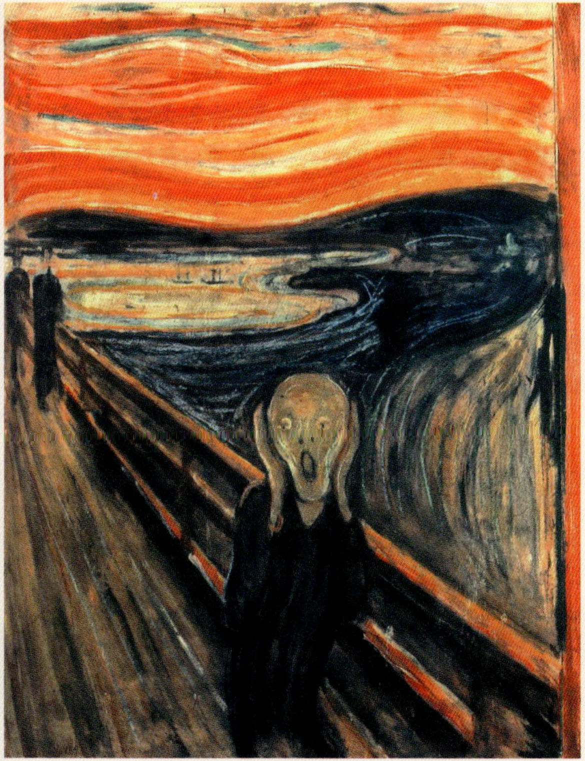

Edvard Munch, *The Scream*, 1893.

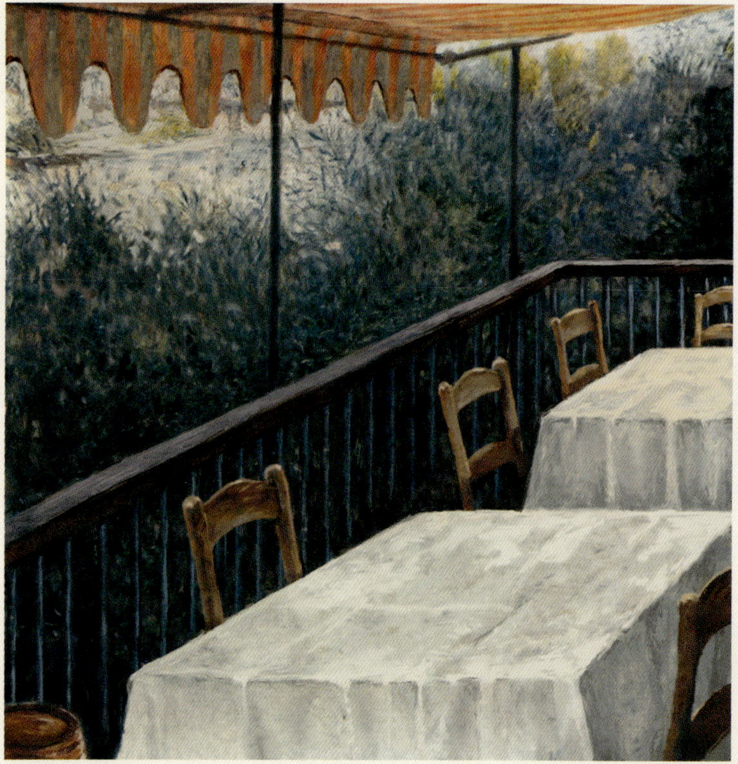

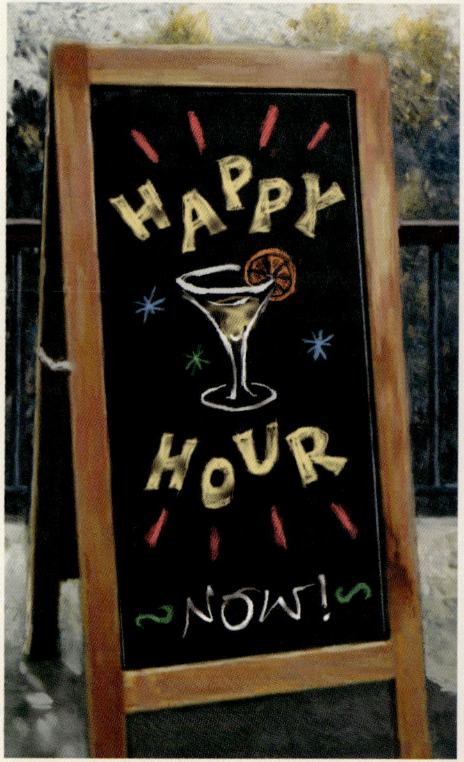
HAPPY
HOUR
NOW!

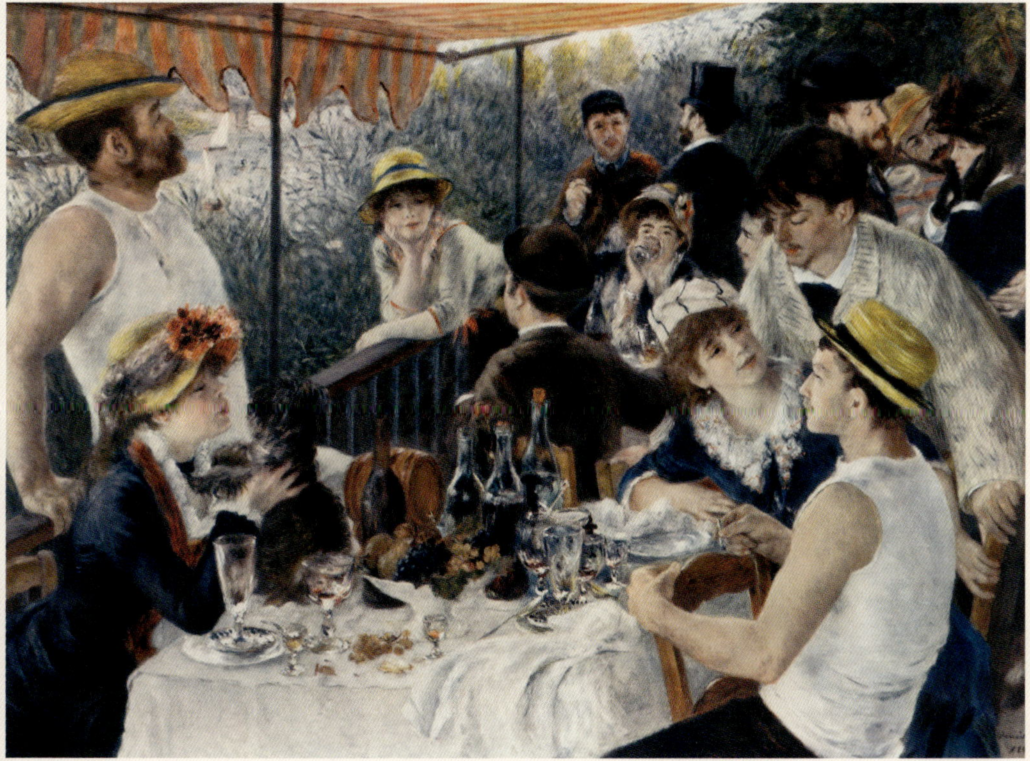

Auguste Renoir, *Luncheon of the Boating Party*, 1881.

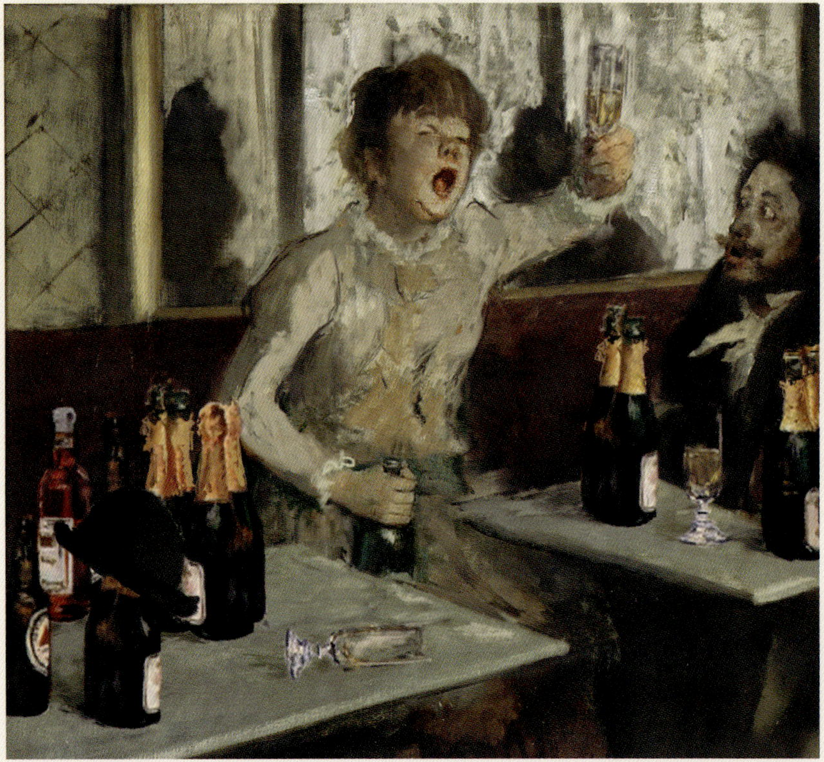

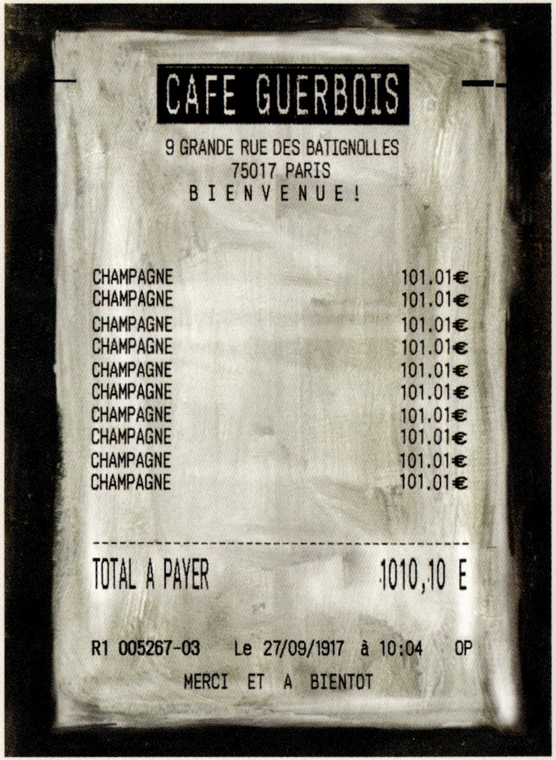
CAFE GUERBOIS
9 GRANDE RUE DES BATIGNOLLES
75017 PARIS
B I E N V E N U E !
CHAMPAGNE 101.01€
CHAMPAGNE 101.01€
CHAMPAGNE 101.01€
CHAMPAGNE 101.01€
CHAMPAGNE 101.01€
CHAMPAGNE 101.01€
CHAMPAGNE 101.01€
CHAMPAGNE 101.01€
CHAMPAGNE 101.01€
CHAMPAGNE 101.01€
TOTAL A PAYER 1010,10 E
R1 005267-03 Le 27/09/1917 à 10:04 OP
MERCI ET A BIENTOT

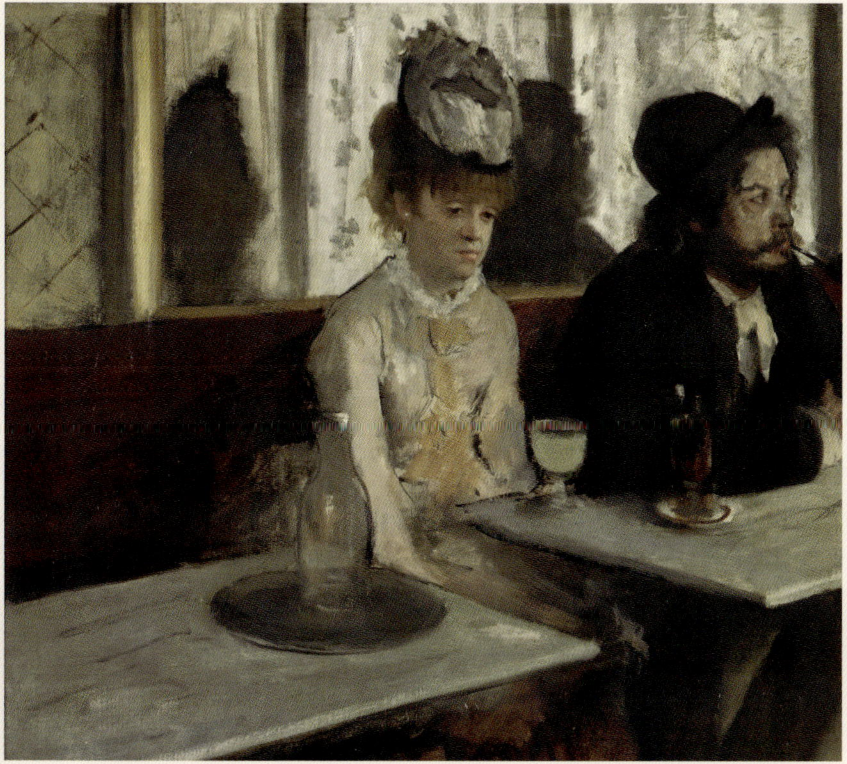

Edgar Degas, *Absinthe*, 1875-1876.

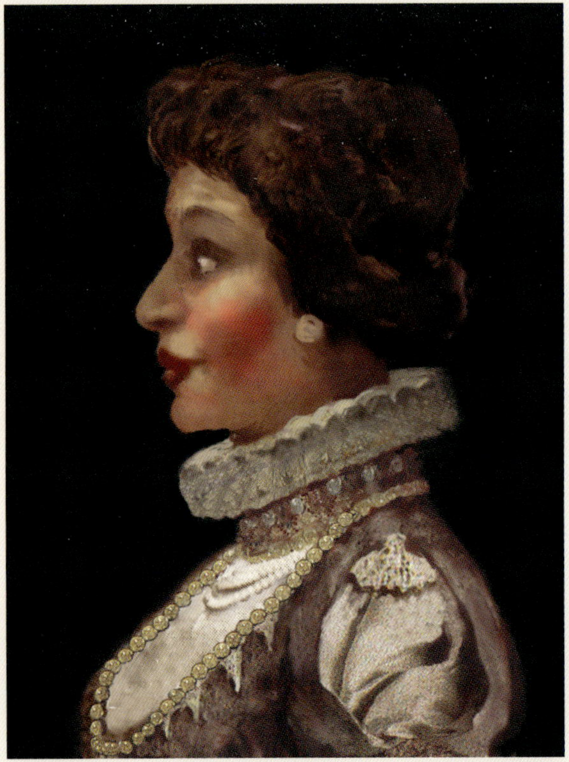

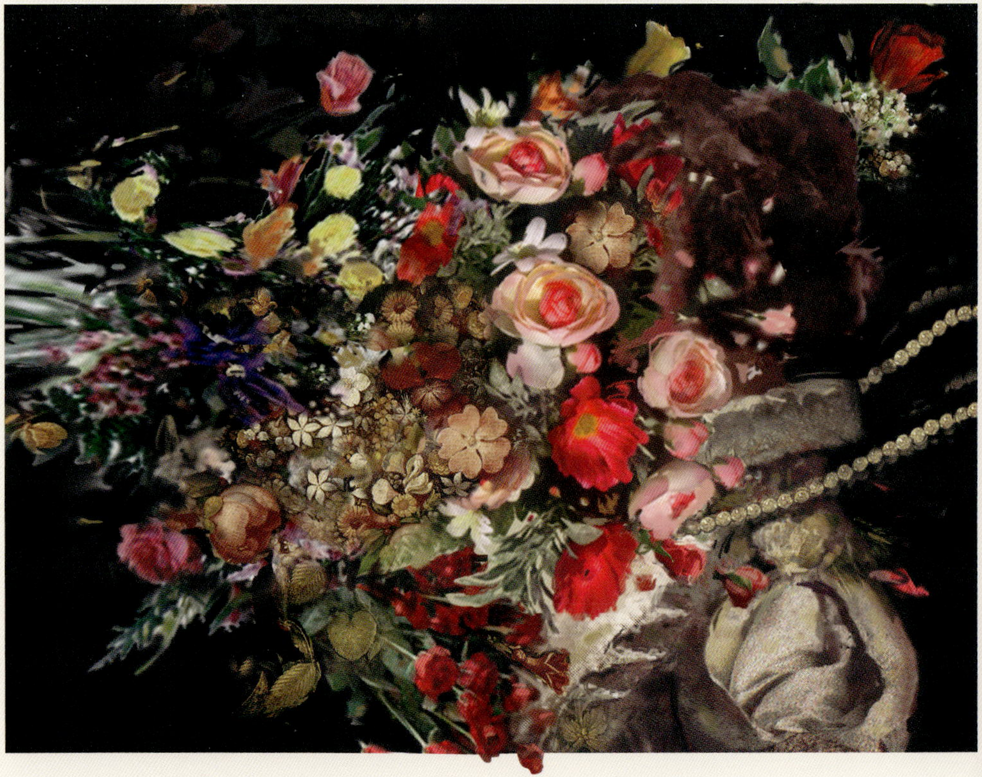

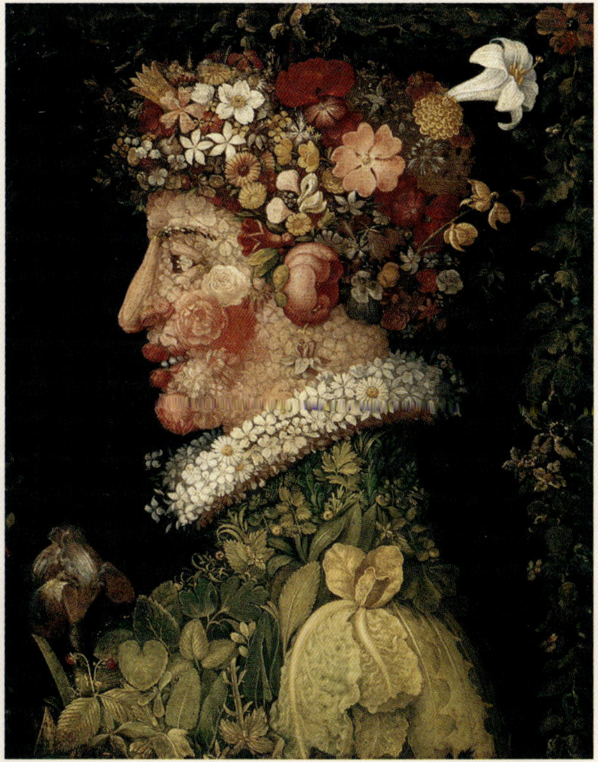

Giuseppe Arcimboldo, *Spring*, 1573.

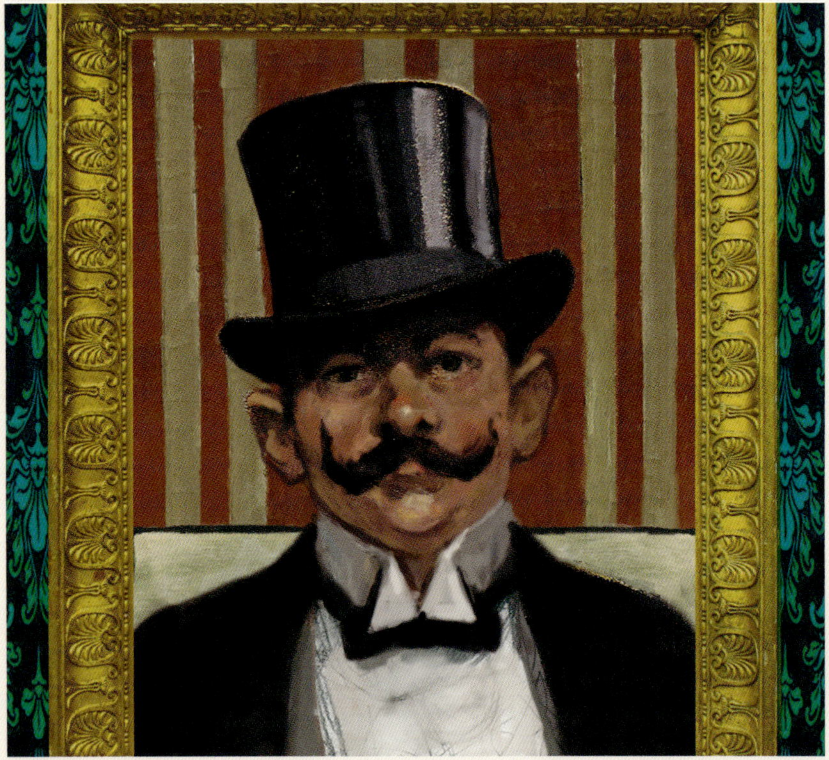

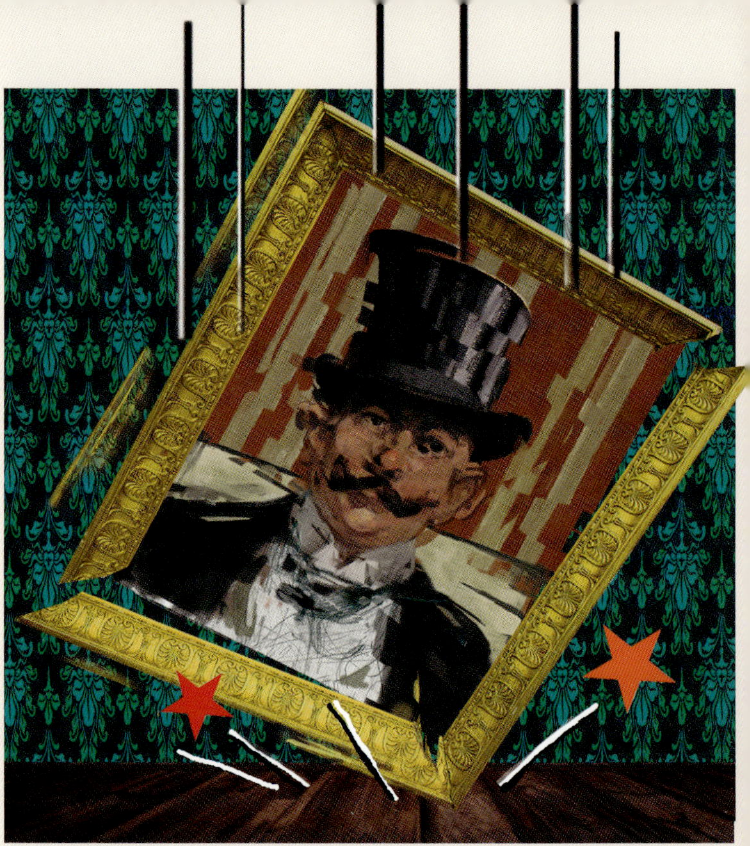

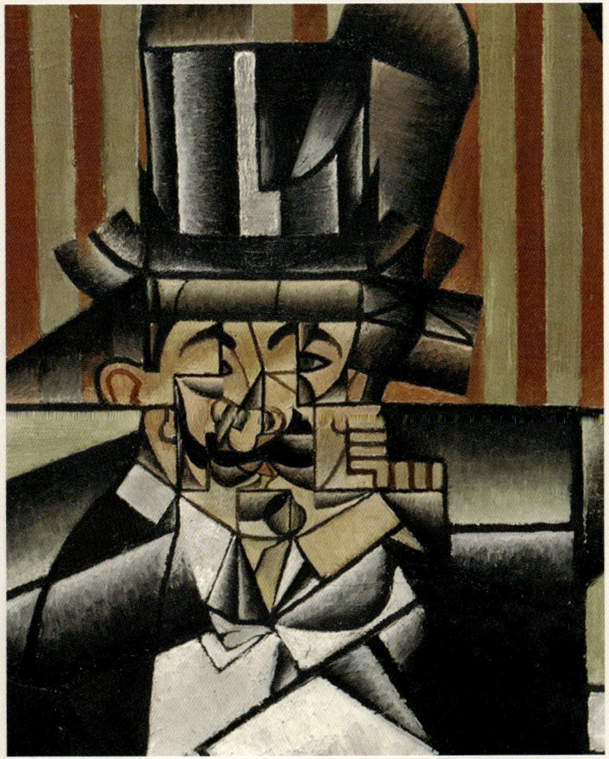

Juan Gris, *Man in the Café*, 1912 (detail).

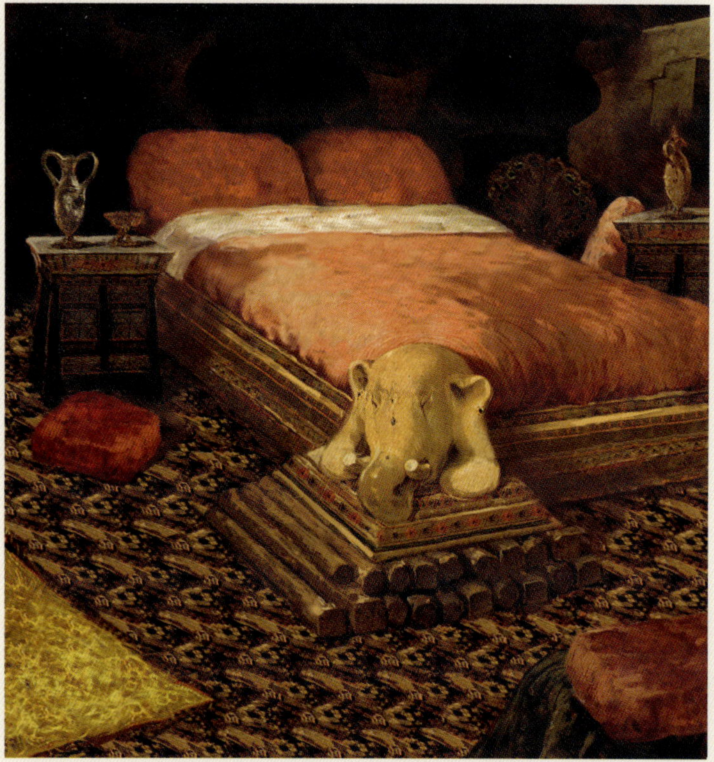

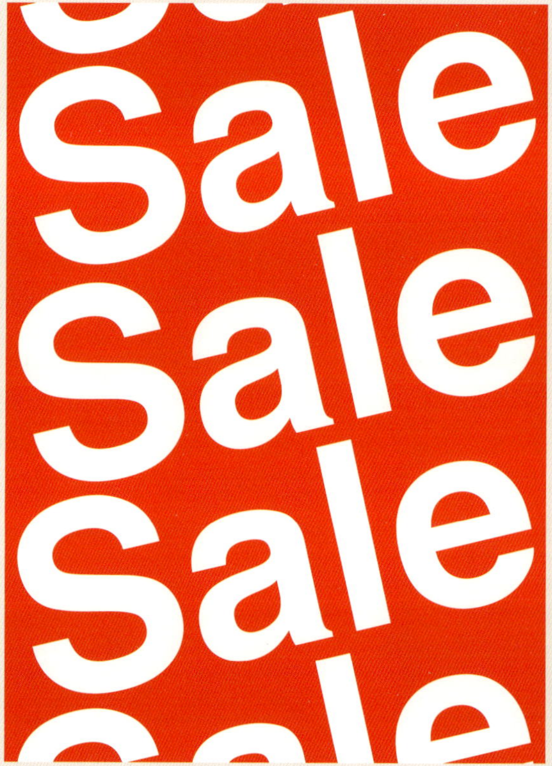
Sale
Sale
Sale

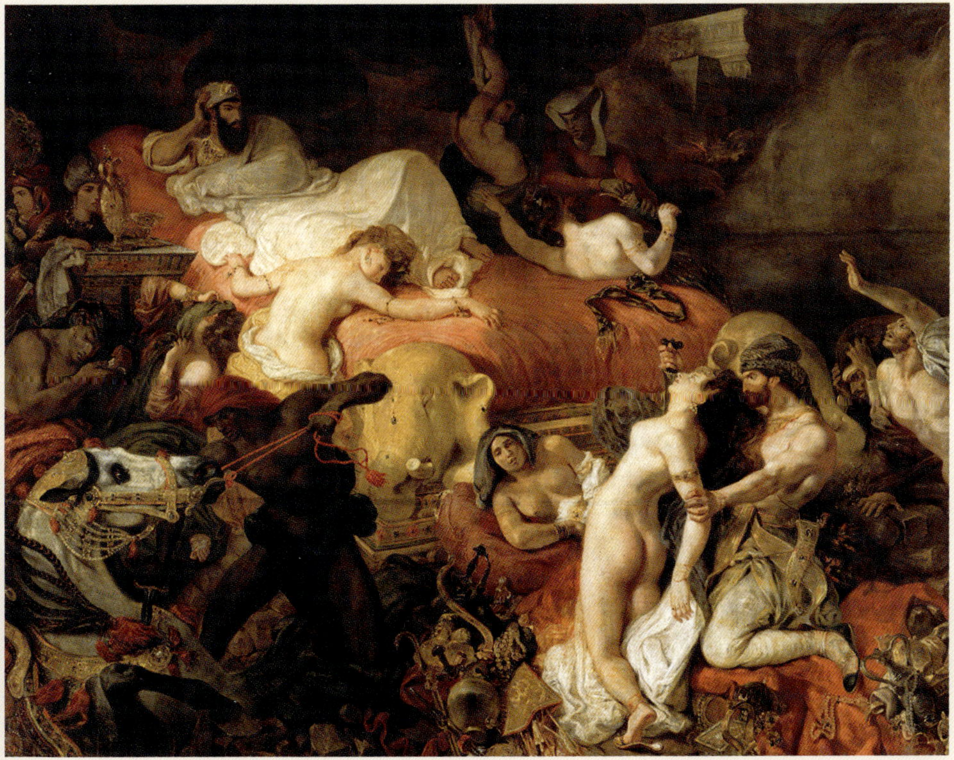

Eugène Delacroix, *The Death of Sardanapalus*, 1827.

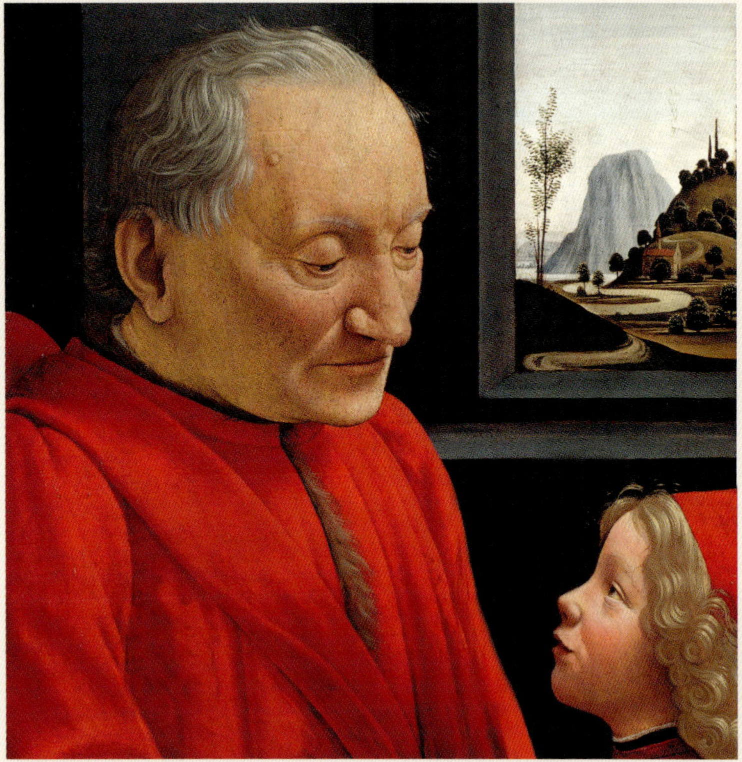

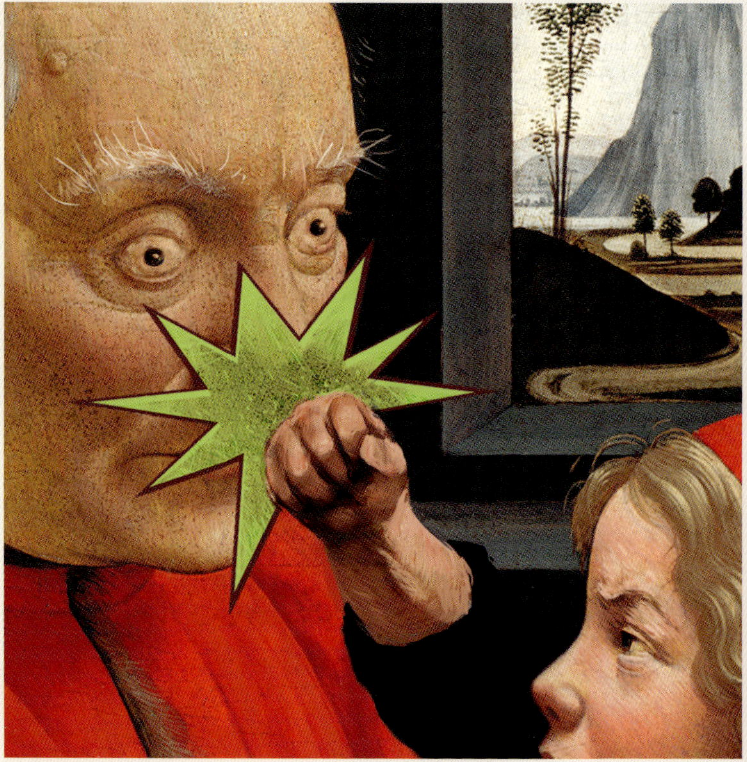

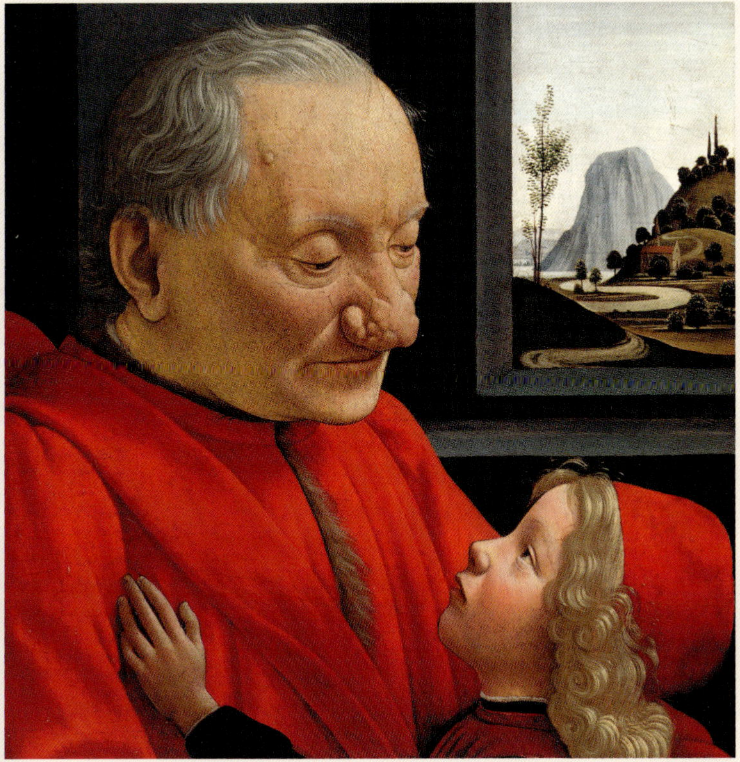

Domenico Ghirlandaio, *An Old Man and His Grandson*, c. 1490.

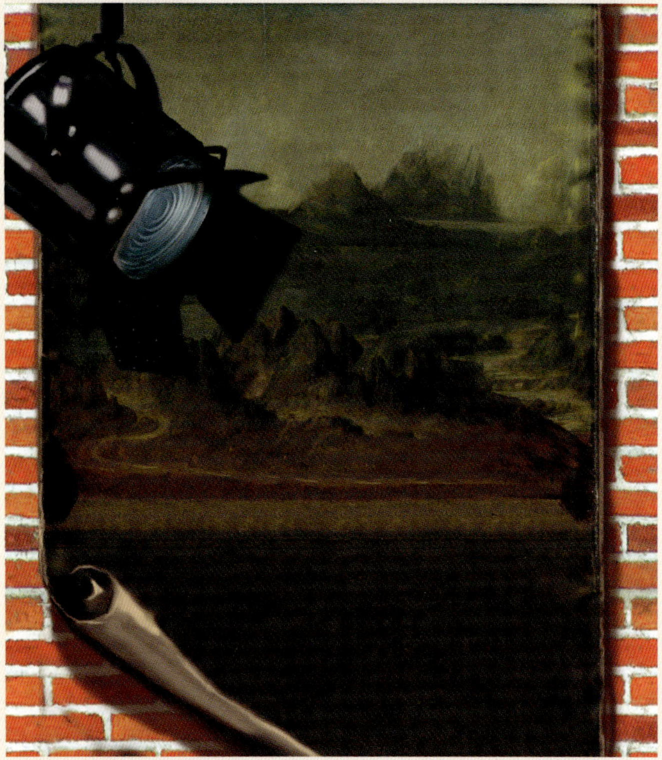

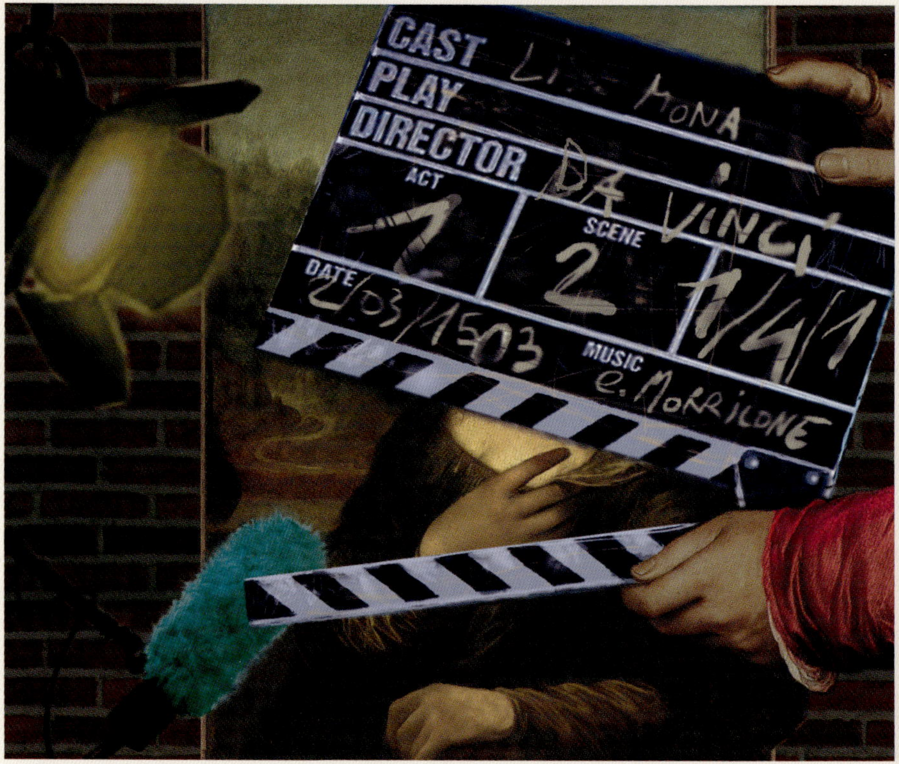

CAST
PLAY
DIRECTOR
ACT
SCENE
DATE
MUSIC

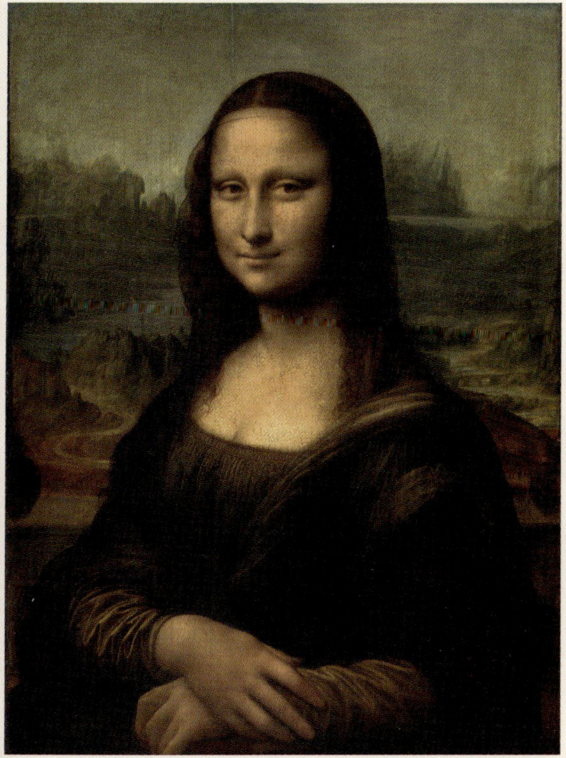

Leonardo da Vinci, *Mona Lisa*, 1503-1506.

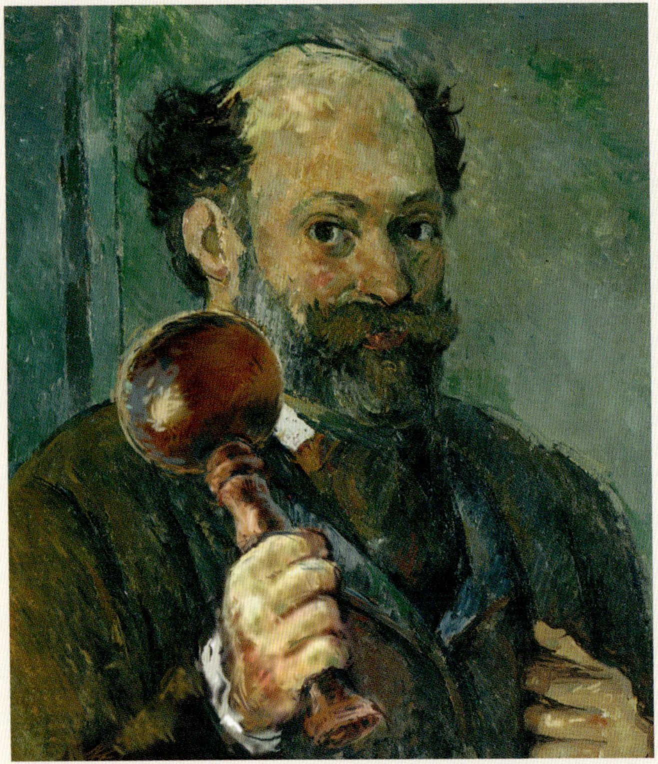

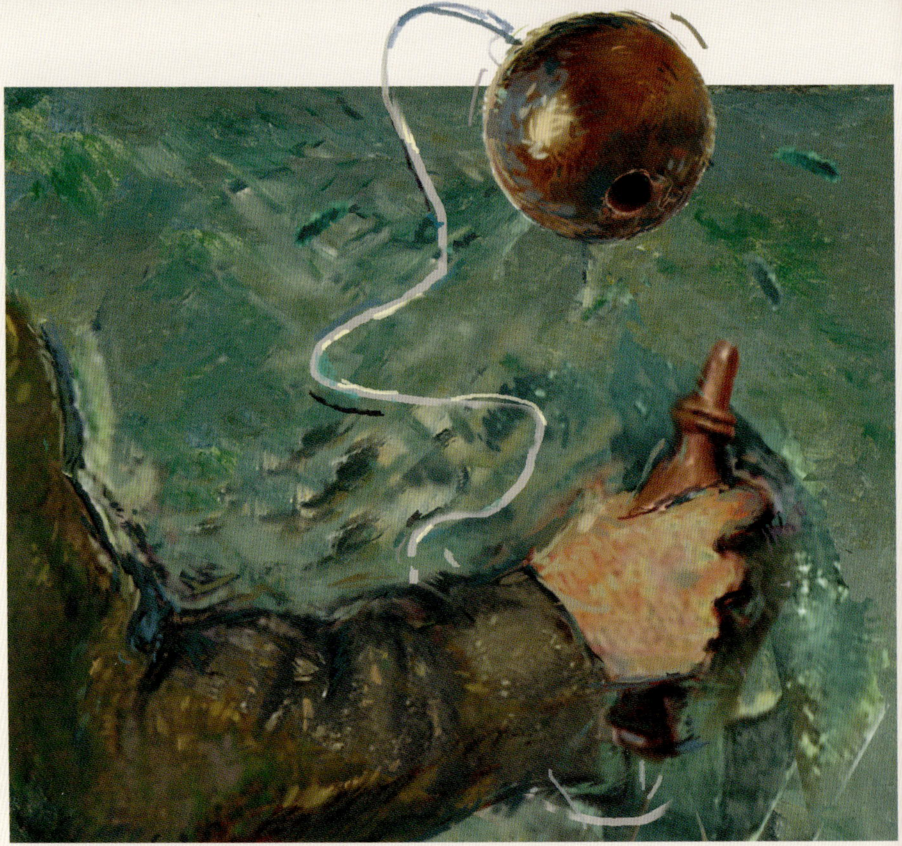

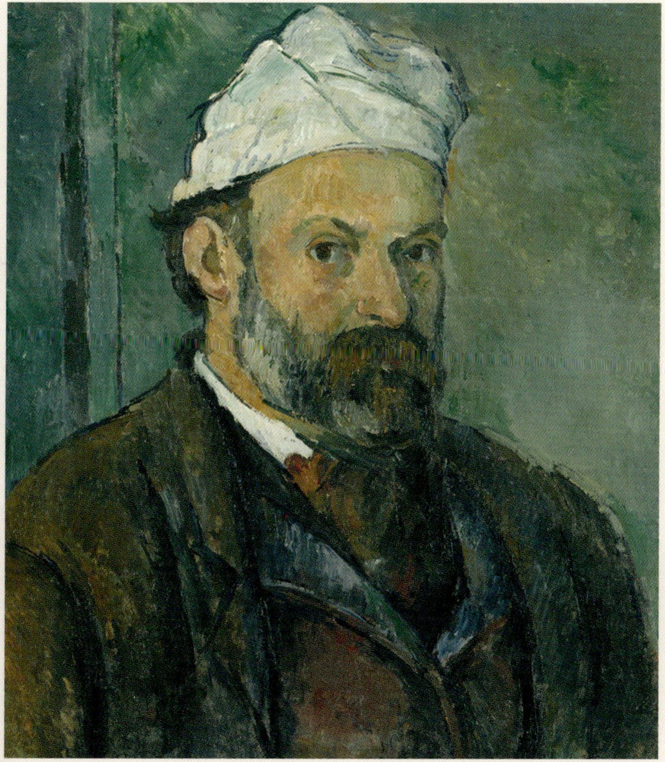

Paul Cézanne, *Self Portrait*, c. 1878-1880.

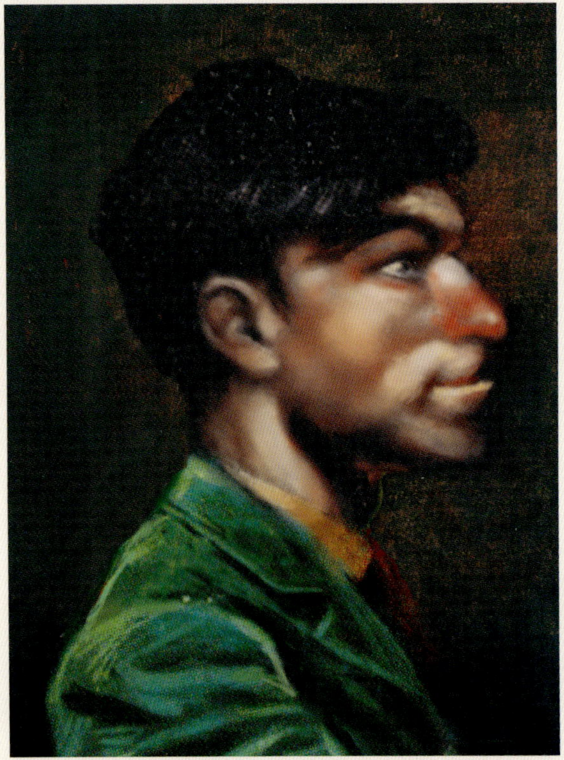

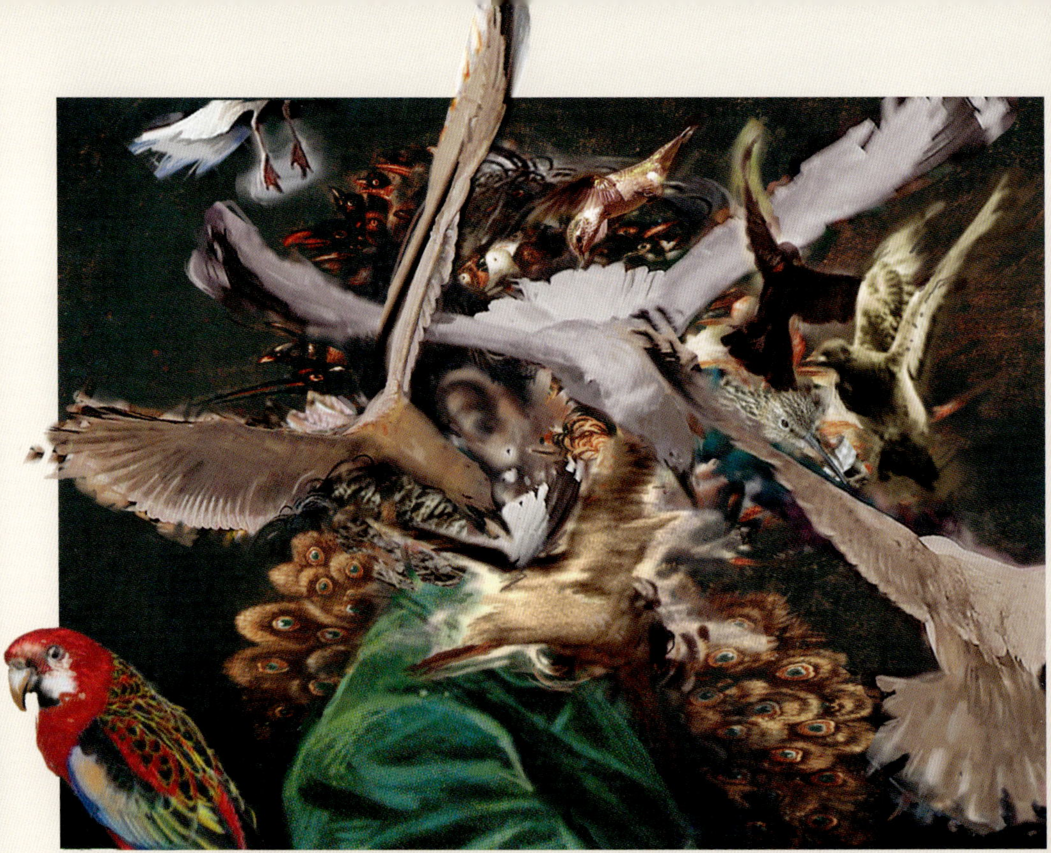

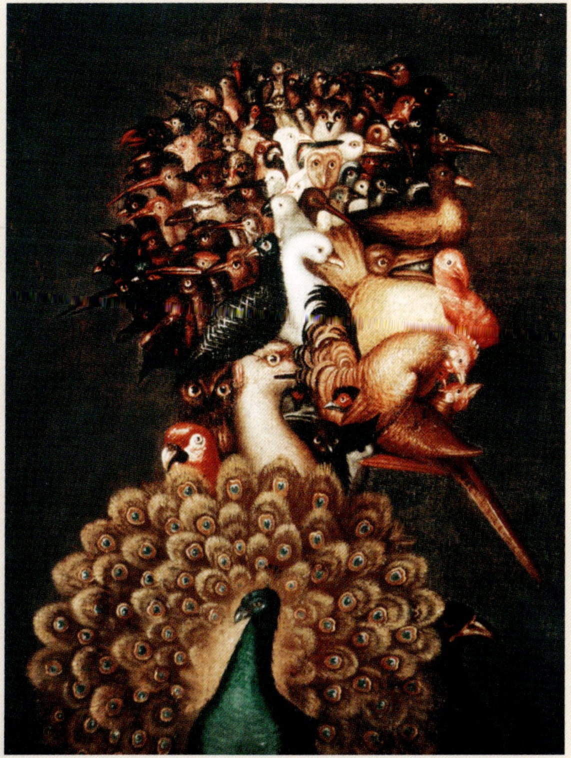

Giuseppe Arcimboldo, *Air*, c. 1580.

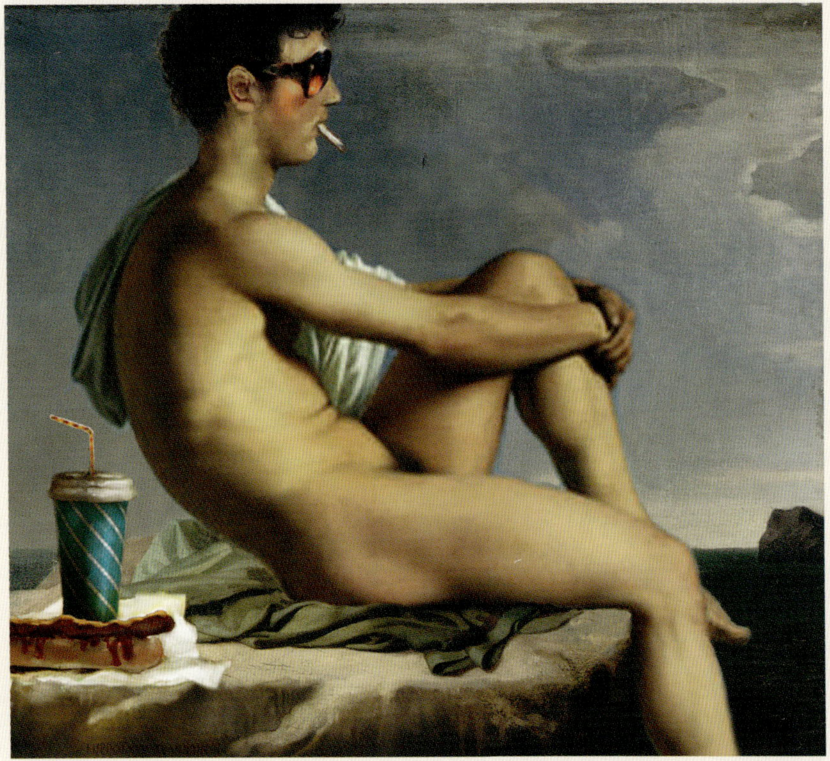

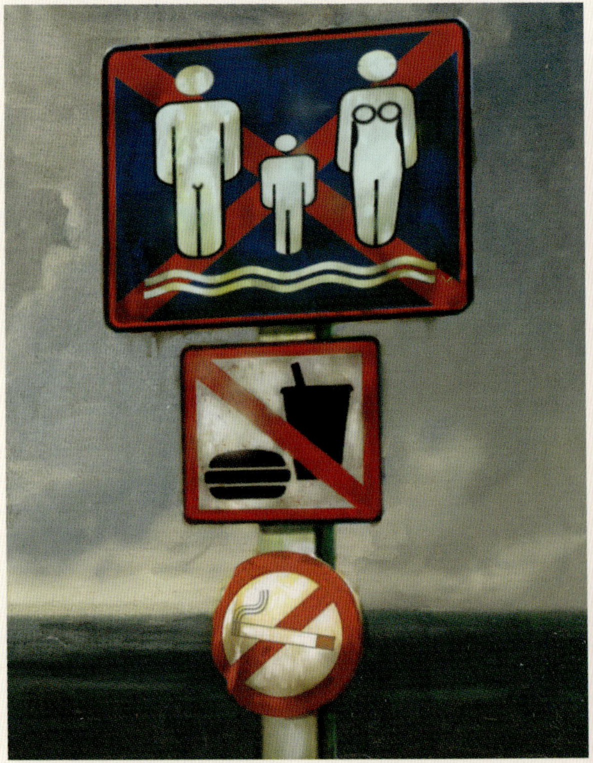

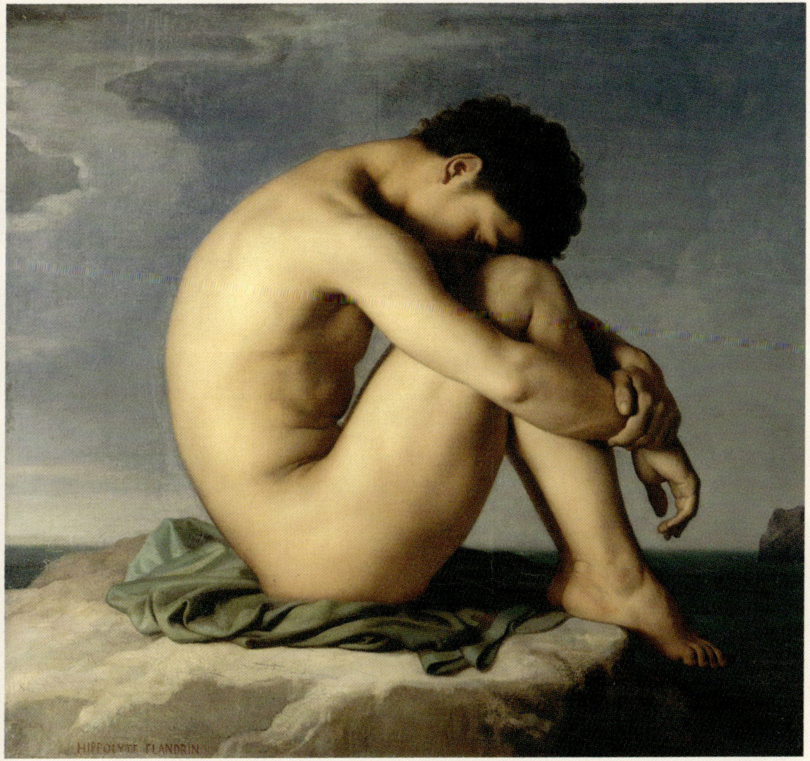

Hippolyte Flandrin, *Young Man by the Sea*, 1836.

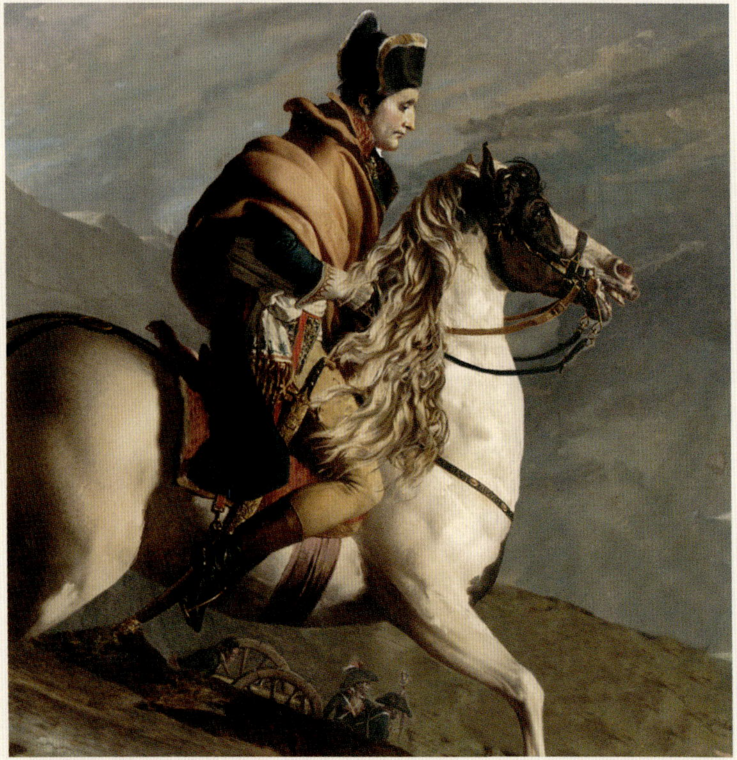

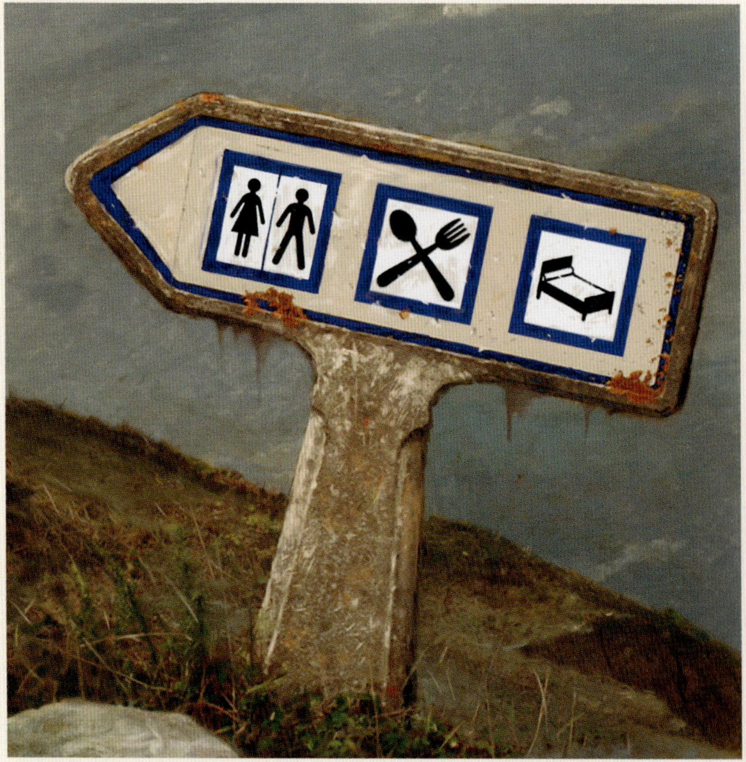

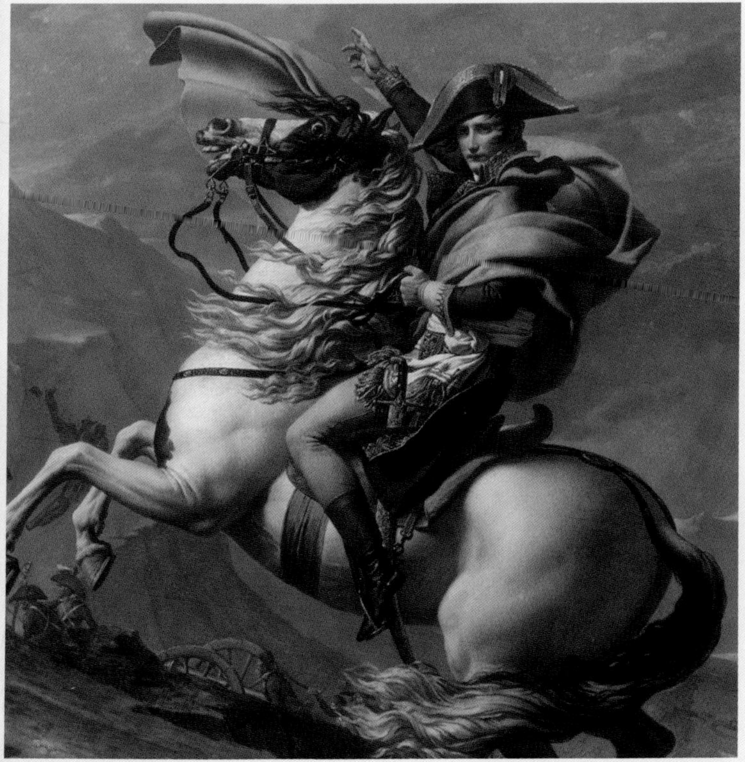

Jacques-Louis David, *Napoleon Crossing the Alps*, 1800.

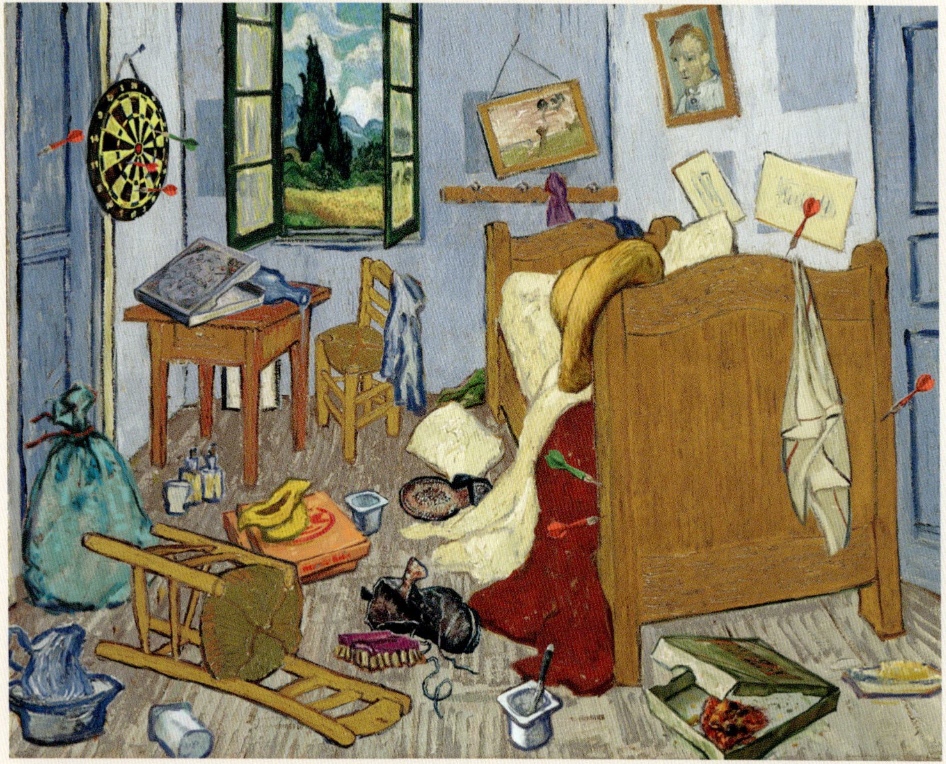

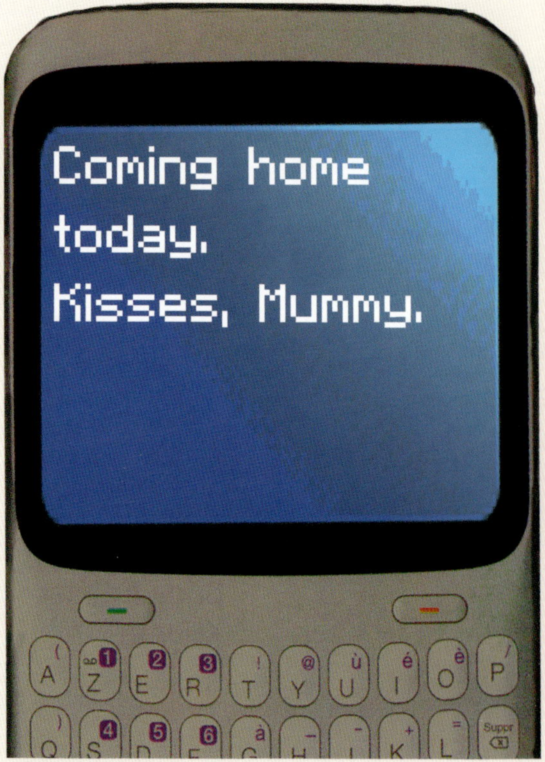
Coming home
today.
Kisses, Mummy.

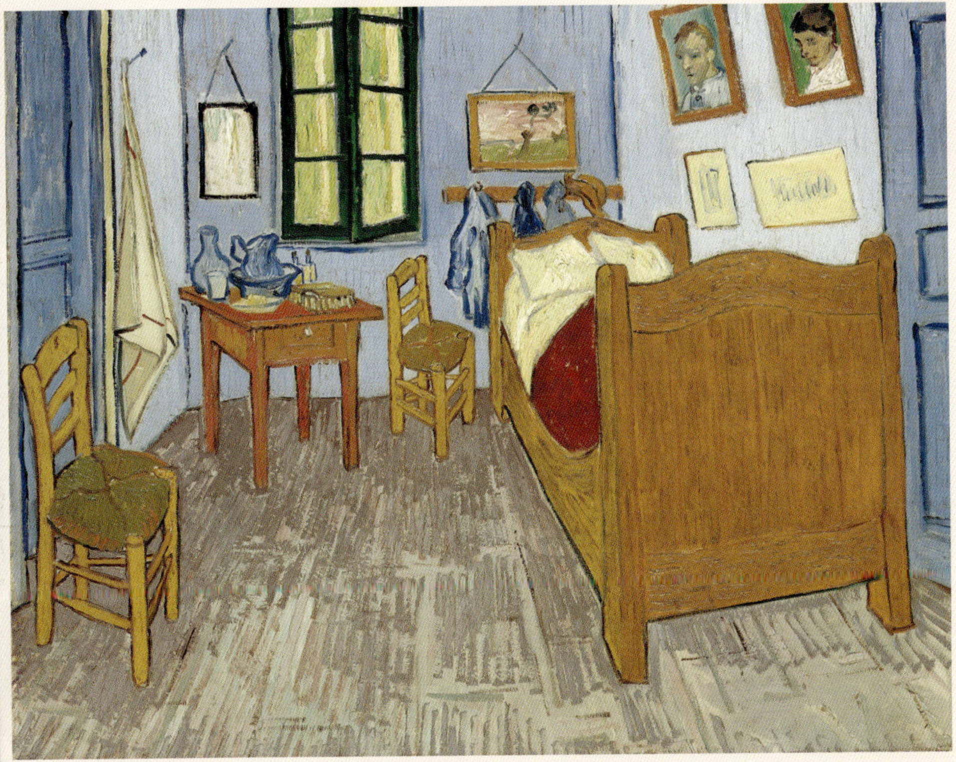

Vincent Van Gogh, *Bedroom in Arles*, 1889.

● Gustave Courbet, *The Desperate Man*, 1841.
Private Collection
© Akg-images / Archives CDA

● Jean Fouquet, *Virgin and Child Surrounded by Angels*, 1452.
Royal Museum of Fine Arts, Antwerp, Belgium.
© Photo Scala, Florence

● Giuseppe Arcimboldo, *Water*, 1566.
Kunsthistorisches Museum, Vienna, Austria
© Akg-images / E. Lessing

● Piero della Francesca, *Federico III da Montefeltro*, 1464-1466.
Uffizi Gallery, Florence, Italy
© Akg-images / E. Lessing

● Claude Monet, *Rouen Cathedral: The Portal in the Sunlight*, 1893.
Musée d'Orsay, Paris, France
© Photo Scala, Florence

● Paul Delaroche, *Napoleon I at Fontainebleau on 31st March 1814*, 1840.
Musée de l'Armée, Paris, France
© Paris - Musée de l'Armée, dist. RMN / image Musée de l'Armée

● Rembrandt, *The Raising of Lazarus*, c. 1630.
Los Angeles County Museum of Art (LACMA), USA
© Digital Image Museum Associates/LACMA/Art Resource NY/Scala, Florence

● Giuseppe Arcimboldo, *Fire*, 1566.
Kunsthistorisches Museum, Vienna, Austria
© Akg-images / E. Lessing

● Francisco de Goya, *The Clothed Maja*, 1800-1803.
Museo del Prado, Madrid, Spain
© Photo Scala, Florence

● Francisco de Goya, *The Nude Maja*, 1800-1803.
Museo del Prado, Madrid, Spain
© Photo Scala, Florence

● Edvard Munch, *The Scream*, 1893.
The National Gallery, Oslo, Norway
© Akg-images / E. Lessing
© The Munch-Museum / The Munch-Ellingsen Group - ADAGP, Paris, 2012

● Auguste Renoir, *Luncheon of the Boating Party*, 1881.
Phillips Collection, Washington, USA
© Akg-images

● Edgar Degas, *Absinthe*, 1875-1876.
Musée d'Orsay, Paris, France
© RMN (Musée d'Orsay) / H. Lewandowski

● Giuseppe Arcimboldo, *Spring*, 1573.
The Louvre, Paris, France
© RMN / J.-G. Berizzi

● Juan Gris, *Man in the Café*, 1912 (detail).
Philadelphia Museum of Art, Philadelphia, USA
© Photo The Philadelphia Museum of Art/Art Resource/ Scala, Florence

● Eugène Delacroix, *The Death of Sardanapalus*, 1827.
The Louvre, Paris, France
© RMN / H. Lewandowski

● Domenico Ghirlandaio, *An Old Man and His Grandson*, c. 1490.
The Louvre, Paris, France
© RMN / H. Lewandowski

● Leonardo da Vinci, *Mona Lisa*, 1503-1506.
The Louvre, Paris, France
© RMN / H. Lewandowski / T. Le Mage

● Paul Cézanne, *Self Portrait*, c. 1878-1880.
Neue Pinakothek, Munich, Germany
© BPK, Berlin, Dist. RMN / image BStGS

● Giuseppe Arcimboldo, *Air*, c. 1580.
Private Collection (Dreyfus Bank), Basel, Switzerland
© Akg-images / E. Lessing

● Hippolyte Flandrin, *Young Man by the Sea*, 1836.
The Louvre, Paris, France
© RMN / D. Arnaudet

● Jacques-Louis David, *Napoleon Crossing the Alps*, 1800.
Château de Malmaison, Rueil-Malmaison, France
© RMN / G. Blot

● Vincent Van Gogh, *Bedroom in Arles*, 1889.
Musée d'Orsay, Paris, France
© RMN (Musée d'Orsay) / H. Lewandowski

First published in English 2013
by SelfMadeHero
5 Upper Wimpole Street
London W1G 6BP
www.selfmadehero.com

Art by Alexis Lemoine
Script by Sylvain Coissard
Graphic design and lay-outs by Loïc Le Gall
(Le Gall & Chassagnard)
Editorial & Production Manager: Lizzie Kaye
Sales & Marketing Manager: Sam Humphrey
Publishing Director: Emma Hayley
With thanks to: Nick de Somogyi & Guillaume Rater

A CIP record for this book is available from the British Library

ISBN: 978-1-906838-71-3

10 9 8 7 6 5 4 3 2 1

Printed and bound in China